STRANGER THAN FICTION

The Life of William Kiffin

B. A. RAMSBOTTOM

GH00631111

GOSPEL STANDARD TRUST PUBLICATIONS

1989

7 Brackendale Grove, Harpenden,
Herts. AL5 3EL, England.

ACKNOWLEDGEMENTS

The author wishes to express appreciation for help in his researches from the Bodleian Library, Oxford; The Evangelical Library, London; Regent's Park College, Oxford; The Guildhall Library, London; Mrs. Winnie Hart of Hove; Mr. Stephen Pickles of Oxford; and especially to Mrs. H. M. Parish for her painstaking work in preparing the script for the press.

ISBN 0 903556 82 0

*Printed in Great Britain
by Flair Press Ltd. Northampton*

CONTENTS

The cover photograph is a view of the River Thames in London from a painting by Carl Neumann.

Ridgwood Sculpt

William Kiffin.

Ætat 50, Anno, 1667.

From an original Painting.

In the Possession of the Revd Richd Frost, Dunmow.

Publish'd Feby 1, 1809, by Maxwell & Wilson, Skinner Street.

LIST OF EVENTS

If it had not been the Lord who was on our side, now may Israel say;

If it had not been the Lord who was on our side, when men rose up against us:

Then they had swallowed us up quick, when their wrath was kindled against us:

Then the waters had overwhelmed us, the stream had gone over our soul:

Then the proud waters had gone over our soul.

Blessed be the Lord, who hath not given us as a prey to their teeth.

Our soul is escaped as a bird out of the snare of the fowlers: the snare is broken, and we are escaped.

Our help is in the name of the Lord, who made heaven and earth.

Psalm 124

CHAPTER 1

Stranger than Fiction

It has often been said that truth is stranger than fiction. But what writer of the most extravagant fiction could have thought up such a life as that of William Kiffin? A poor orphan becoming one of the wealthiest merchants in the country; dearly loved and bitterly hated; a preacher and pastor for sixty years yet a Member of Parliament; a confidant of two monarchs and yet in and out of prison; accused of the most fantastic plots yet remarkably delivered; and at last dying quietly at home in a ripe old age. Such is the life of Kiffin!

William Kiffin's two biographers, writing many years ago, both seem impressed by this fact of truth and fiction — as a well-known poet aptly put it: "'Tis strange — but true; for truth is always strange; stranger than fiction, if it could be told." One saw a remarkable resemblance between Kiffin and the legendary Dick Whittington; the other thought that Sir Walter Scott's famous novel *Peveril of the Peak* was based upon Kiffin's life! No doubt there is more weight in Joseph Ivimey's comparison of Kiffin to Joseph, David and Mordecai.

But this is not fiction. Here is a godly man, called by God to preach, who in days of deep adversity and amazing prosperity honoured the Lord, "choosing rather to suffer affliction with the people of God, than to enjoy the pleasures of sin for a season." What earthly honours this man might have had if he had so chosen!

If there are many strange things connected with the life of William Kiffin, the strangest of all is this: Why is it that a life both so remarkable and interesting is so little known today? Mention Kiffin, and there is a bewildered frown, or the innocent question: "Who was Kiffin?" We dare not begin to suggest why this should be so; but, sadly, it is. Yet begin to speak of Kiffin's life and immediately interest is aroused — though sometimes the incredulous hint that perhaps things are being exaggerated.

Rather over a hundred years ago, G. Holden Pike writing in *London's Ancient Meeting Houses* expressed the same surprise — that Kiffin was so little known. But he also expressed his desire that one day "a good life" of Kiffin might appear. Well, this is an account of the life of William Kiffin. Only the reader can decide what epithet it deserves.

Interestingly, Kiffin himself believed that there was great value in reading the lives of God's people, and also that it is eminently scriptural to write them. When asked to write an "Epistle to the Reader" for *The Life and Death of Hanserd Knollys*, he wrote:

"It was the special charge God gave to His people of old that the many signal providences and mercies that they had received from Him should by them be recorded and left to their children's children, to the end that the memorial of His goodness might cause them to love and fear His name; and therefore they are required to bless the Lord from the fountain of Israel, from the very beginning of all His favours towards them. It is no small favour the servants of God are made partakers of that His people of old have left so many testimonies of the gracious goodness and providences of God towards them; being a means to strengthen the faith of His people, in a dependency upon Him, in all those variety of dispensations that do attend them in this world: that whatever troubles they meet withal in this life, they may know that God deals no otherwise with them than He hath done to those that formerly have feared His name; and may be comforted with the same comforts and supports which His servants formerly have received from God."

CHAPTER 2

Early Days

1625 was a terrible year in London. One of those dreadful plagues which again and again had troubled England (thought to be carried by black rats) had again visited the capital, and it is estimated that about a third of the population was wiped out.

Among those suffering from the plague was a nine year old boy. He had no less than six of those deadly plague boils — yet, miraculously, he recovered. That young boy was William Kiffin. God had a purpose for his life so, to use the well-worn saying, he was "immortal till his work was done." Sadly though, both his parents perished in the plague.

Nothing is known about his background and ancestors, but the name "Kiffin" suggests that his family had originally come from Wales — "Kiffin" signifying "a borderer" in Welsh. He himself sometimes spelled his name "Kiffen" and sometimes "Kiffin."

William Kiffin's life (1616-1701) almost spans one of the most turbulent centuries in English history. Gunpowder Plot, the appearance of the authorized version of the Bible and the voyage of the Pilgrim Fathers were all recent memories in that fateful plague year — which was the year, also, when Charles I succeeded his father on the throne.

So Kiffin's life was to witness the Civil War, the execution of the King, the Protectorate of Oliver Cromwell, the Restoration of the Monarchy and the attendant bitter persecution of nonconformists under

9

Charles II, reaching to the days of toleration following the Glorious Revolution, and not ending till the turn of the century.

What important years these were! Recently they have been described as "the most turbulent, seditious and factious years of recorded English history." And Kiffin is surely one of the most remarkable and interesting men of his age, from any point of view.

Sadly the young orphan's early days were not easy. What relatives and friends he had seemed more concerned to avail themselves of his parents' property than to look after the parentless child.

At the age of 13 he was bound apprentice as a brewer's clerk in London. All the old accounts speak of him as being apprenticed to the celebrated John Lilburne but obviously there is some error here. Lilburne himself was only a year or so older than William Kiffin so could have been but 14 or 15 himself at the time. It seems more likely that they were apprentices together.

John Lilburne was one of the most turbulent men during that turbulent age. Leader of the Levellers (who sought to abolish the monarchy and the House of Lords), he was a republican agitator who spoke and published against Charles I, fought against him as a lieutenant-colonel in the Parliamentary army, and later opposed Cromwell's government. On one occasion when put in the pillory by the Star Chamber, he fulminated so against the bishops, and his language was so insolent, that his persecutors were compelled to gag him. On another occasion, after enduring terrible sufferings in gaol, he escaped by setting the gaol on fire! It was said that "if the world were emptied of all but John Lilburne, Lilburne would quarrel with John, and John with Lilburne." He certainly managed to enter into most of the controversies of his day. Whipped, pilloried, imprisoned, banished, he survived all and at last died in peace — as a Quaker!

This, then, was William Kiffin's companion at the brewery. "A very mean calling," Kiffin later described his situation, and he was far from happy. Because of his conditions, he became quite melancholy, and after a year or more he resolved to quit.

Very early one morning, before anyone was awake, young Kiffin crept from the place where he lodged, determined never to return. It was, of course, a serious thing for an apprentice to break with his master, but the poor boy felt he could stand it no longer.

Wandering aimlessly through the city, he came to St. Antholin's Church. These were the days of the Puritans and to his amazement he observed people flocking into the church even at that early hour. Without any particular purpose Kiffin followed them in; he had no special religious interest, but what else was there to do?

The preacher was Thomas Foxley, a learned and zealous Puritan who later suffered much under Archbishop Laud. The subject was the Fifth Commandment: "Honour thy father and thy mother." Most remarkably the preacher dealt with the commandment as meaning the obedience of servants to their masters just as much as children to their parents. Much of what was said the poor boy could not understand, but he thought that the minister must know all about his running away, and was speaking personally to him!

Accordingly William Kiffin hurried back to his lodgings as quickly as he could. And no one had missed him! It was still early — so creeping back into the house, he was able to carry on as if nothing had happened.

But all this had left a deep impression on his mind. From now on he became a regular hearer of the Puritan preachers.

CHAPTER 3

The Puritan Preachers

Being now deeply impressed by the reality of divine things, William Kiffin began to have serious thoughts. Going back again to St. Antholin's, the place where God had met him, he heard a minister named John Norton, a man who spent whole days in prayer and who was described as "another Augustine." Norton's text was: "There is no peace saith my God to the wicked" (Isa. 57.21). He clearly showed what true peace is, and insisted that no one could ever obtain it "without an interest in Christ."

> "Which sermon" (wrote Kiffin) "took very great impression on my heart, being convinced I had not that peace, and how to obtain an interest in Christ Jesus I knew not; which occasioned great perplexity in my soul. I every day saw myself more and more sinful and vile. Pray I could not, nor believe in Jesus Christ I could not, and thought myself shut up in unbelief; and, although I desired to mourn under the sense of my sin, yet I saw there was no proportion of sorrow suitable to that evil nature which I found working strongly in my soul. As the only thing I could do I took up resolutions to attend upon the most powerful preaching, which accordingly I did; by means of which I found some relief (many times) from the sense of a possibility that, notwithstanding my sinful state, I might at last obtain mercy. I resolved also to leave sin; but, although to will was present sometimes, yet how to perform I had no power."

Here, then, was this boy, about 15 years old, feeling himself a sinner, and attending diligently to the most powerful preaching he could find.

After some time he went to hear John Davenport, "a princely preacher" (as he was described), at the church in Coleman Street. At this time Mr. Davenport was very fervent and even vehement in his preaching. On this occasion he preached from the beautiful text: "And the blood of Jesus Christ His Son cleanseth us from all sin" (1 John 1.7). He spoke of the wonderful efficacy of the blood of Christ both to pardon and cleanse from sin, and answered many objections which an unbelieving heart would raise against the full satisfaction which Christ made for sinners.

"Many of which" (says Kiffin) "I found to be such that I made in my own heart: as the sense of unworthiness, and willingness to be better before I would come to Christ for life, with many other of the like kind. This sermon was of great satisfaction to my soul; and I thought I found my heart greatly to close with the riches and freeness of grace, which God held forth to poor sinners in Jesus Christ. I found my fears to vanish, and my heart filled with love to Jesus Christ. I saw sin viler than ever, and my heart more abhorring it."

Soon afterwards, he heard Mr. Norton again, this time from Luke 1.69: "And hath raised up an horn of salvation for us in the house of His servant David." Kiffin wrote of this occasion:

"He showed that Jesus Christ was mightily accomplished with power and ability to save His people. My faith was exceedingly strengthened in the fulness of that satisfaction which Jesus Christ had given to the Father for poor sinners, and was enabled to believe my interest therein. Then I found some ability to pray, and to meditate upon the riches of this grace; so that I could say with David, 'When I awake, I am still with Thee.' I found the power of inbred corruption scatter, and my heart set on fire with holy love to Christ."

Interestingly, both these ministers, so blessed to William Kiffin, soon after emigrated to New England in North

America, Norton becoming minister at Boston and Davenport at Stanford. The testimony concerning the latter following his death was: "A man never yet praised enough, and never to be named without praise."

These, then, were the kind of preachers Kiffin heard.

Like many young converts, Kiffin did not yet really know himself and the deceitfulness of his heart. He could not understand older Christians complaining so much about the strength of sin in their hearts. "I thought I should never find the power and strength of sin that they found daily in their souls."

> "In this frame" (he said) "of peace and rest, I continued for near three months, rejoicing in the grace of God, and was ready to say that by His favour He had made my mountain so strong that I should never be removed. But a new storm began to arise in my soul; for under the comfort and peace I enjoyed, I thought the power of inbred corruption had been so broken within me that I should never have found it prevail over me any more. I began to feel my confidence in God to abate, my comforts to lessen, and the motions of sin to revive with greater strength than ever. In every duty I performed, my heart was so carnal that it were a burden to me, and by reason thereof I was a burden to myself. My comforts were gone, and in all the duties of religion, I was as a man that had no strength; yet durst I not omit the performance of any, having some secret hopes that the Lord would not utterly cast me off in displeasure, although my fears were stronger than my hopes. I was daily questioning whether all that I formerly enjoyed might be any more than such a taste of the good Word of God, and powers of the world to come, as those had enjoyed who nevertheless fell away."

For many weeks this distress of mind continued and the boy was too ashamed to ask anyone about it. He was further troubled, in listening to a conversation, by what he *thought* he heard a godly man say: "The least measure

of true grace is for a man to know that he *has* grace.''
Of course, he had misheard — but understandably his
darkness and distress were increased. He concluded that
he must be destitute of grace.

He received some relief through hearing a sermon
preached by a Mr. Moulin at London-Stone church. This
was probably the French Protestant, Lewis de Moulin, who
became a professor at Cambridge. To his amazement, and
comfort, the preacher dealt with the very point which was
troubling him:

> ''He fell upon that question, what the least measure of
> grace was? and before he gave a positive answer, proved
> that for a man to know he had grace could not be the least
> measure but a very large degree of grace, being a reflex act
> of faith. He then gave several characters of the least measure
> of true grace. I greatly wondered within myself to hear him
> fall upon that which did so greatly and particularly concern
> me, and also found in my own soul some small beginnings
> of those signs of true grace which he laid down. This
> wonderfully relieved my hopes again; God being pleased to
> give me some strength to depend upon His grace more than
> I had received for many weeks before; my resolutions being
> strengthened to follow God, and to wait upon Him in every
> duty, whatsoever His pleasure might be towards me at the
> last.''

He was also greatly encouraged by two passages of
Scripture which were brought to him with great power.
One was Isa. 30.18: ''Therefore will the Lord wait, that
He may be gracious unto you, and therefore will He be
exalted, that He may have mercy upon you: for the Lord
is a God of judgment: blessed are all they that wait for
Him.'' He writes:

> ''Meditation on these words filled me with astonishment
> — that the great God of heaven and earth should reckon
> Himself exalted to show mercy to poor sinners, and to
> encourage such to wait, and not be discouraged.''

He was brought to feel that as God is a God of judgment, so He knows the best time to give longing souls what they are waiting for.

The other word was Isa. 50.10: "Who is among you that feareth the Lord, that obeyeth the voice of His servant, that walketh in darkness, and hath no light? let him trust in the name of the Lord, and stay upon his God." This text was greatly blessed to him in reading the well-known work on the subject by the eminent Puritan divine, Thomas Goodwin, *A Child of Light Walking in Darkness* (a similar work to the sermon by J. C. Philpot preached on the same subject many years later).

Through these two scriptures he was saved from the temptation not to trouble about waiting upon God. Yet another temptation continually harassed him:

> "Yet I was ready to run to my own righteousness; I mean to an expectation of something in myself by which I might get greater victory over sin, and more love to God and His ways, before I should believe in Christ for pardon."

In recording God's dealings with his soul, Kiffin realised on looking back that all his perplexities sprang from his trying to find something *in himself* whereby he might the better approach Christ. Sadly his perplexities were aggravated by one of the special characteristics of some Puritan preaching — not only pressing the necessity of a deep conviction brought about by the preaching of the law but insisting on a rigid standard of experience. (He specially mentions Thomas Hooker's *The Soul's Preparation for Christ*.) Young Kiffin (now about 17 years old) was very deeply convinced of sin, yet, as he examined his own heart with a tender conscience, he thought that he had never been convinced deeply enough. Thus he almost came to conclude that he was deceived and that God had never dealt graciously with him.

But how mysterious is God's sovereignty! About this

time John Goodwin settled in London. Goodwin (not to be confused with the more famous Thomas Goodwin) was a preacher usually regarded with some suspicion. But this was the very man God used to set Kiffin's soul at liberty. His eyes were drawn away from himself to Christ and now he found a sweet resting place.

> "I had for some time seen the want of Christ, and believed that it was by Him only I must expect pardon; and had also seen the worth and excellencies that were in Him above all other objects: so that I now felt my soul to rest upon and trust in Him."

For some time, understandably, he attended the preaching of Mr. Goodwin.

CHAPTER 4

Which Church?

At this time there was true zeal in young William Kiffin's religion. He found there were a few other apprentices he met who like himself were deeply concerned about the things of God. They would meet together at five o'clock in the morning to speak together of their souls' concerns and of the Lord Jesus, and also to pray. Afterwards they would attend the six o'clock lecture at Cornhill or at Christ Church.

What days were these when young, uneducated apprentices would spend their precious spare moments with one desire, to find out more about Christ and His gospel!

William Kiffin writes:

"After a little time, we also read some portion of Scripture, and spoke from it what it pleased God to enable us; wherein I found very great advantage, and by degrees did arrive to some small measure of knowledge. I found the sound of the Scriptures very pleasant and delightful to me, to which I attended as it pleased God to give me an opportunity."

And this seems to be the key to Kiffin's life — his love of the Word of God, and his desire to follow it whatever the cost.

As a number of godly ministers were leaving England because they were dissatisfied with the established Church, Kiffin began to consider the whole subject of nonconformity. Was the state Church scriptural? What did the Word of God teach? He obtained various books and manuscripts and compared them carefully with Scripture.

One thing that struck him was the way in which "God was always jealous of His worship, and had left many examples of His severity on those who had added anything thereunto." He seemed specially affected by the solemn judgments which fell on Nadab and Abihu and on Uzza for departing from God's order.

Yet he felt to know so little and realised that very able ministers did conform to the state Church. So he sought their help — but did not receive any! They seemed to despise his youth and showed "more passion than reason." Perhaps conscience was pricking them. In later years some of them had to condemn the very things they were now upholding.

So William Kiffin had to turn away from man to God. He says, "Finding myself so disappointed of what I had hoped I might have received from them, I was the more provoked to beg earnestly of God to direct me, and searched more closely the Scriptures." Two preachers were a special help to him at this time. One was Jeremiah Burroughs, the well-known author of *The Rare Jewel of Christian Contentment*, a strong advocate for the independency of churches. The other a Mr. Glover (probably John Glover who Cotton Mather lists as one of the New England divines).

Soon after this, Burroughs left for Holland and Glover for New England — where William Kiffin felt that soon he himself would go. However, he had to prove that though "man proposes, God disposes."

So little by little, deeply burdened and concerned, William Kiffin was at last led to become both an Independent and a Baptist — holding firmly the doctrines of free and sovereign grace, and upholding baptism by immersion for believers only, and the necessity of this before coming to the Lord's supper. In other words, by conscience he became a "Strict and Particular Baptist."

The history of the Baptists at this period is somewhat

confused and not as clear as older historians believed. The popular, older account is that when he was 22 years old (in 1638) he joined an Independent church in London under the pastoral care of Henry Jessey. After a time he and some other members united with a Particular Baptist congregation at Wapping (usually counted the first in England), with John Spilsbury as pastor. His third move was when Kiffin himself led an amiable separation to form a second church, the church in Devonshire Square, of which he became pastor until his death. A more modern view is that the church he first joined, Independent then Baptist, was the church where he remained the whole of his life — though again this has been disputed. An ancient document known as ''the Kiffin manuscript'' (though it is not certain that it really was written by Kiffin) has been closely followed, but it can be read in different ways and with different conclusions.*

What is certain is that many years later he wrote:

> ''When it pleased God of His free grace to cause me to make a serious enquiry after Jesus Christ, and to give me some taste of His pardoning love, the sense of which did engage my heart with desires to be obedient to His will in all things, I used all endeavours both by converse with such as were able, and also by diligently searching the Scriptures, with earnest desires of God, that I might be directed in a right way of worship; and after some time concluded that the safest way was to follow the footsteps of the flock (namely) that order laid down by Christ and His apostles, and practised by the primitive Christians in their times, which I found to be: that after conversion they were baptized, added to the church, and continued in the apostles' doctrine, fellowship, breaking of bread and prayer; according to which I thought myself bound to be conformable, and have continued in the profession of the same for these forty years.''

*The matter is discussed by B. R. White in an article: ''How Did William Kiffin Join the Baptists?'' (Baptist Quarterly, Vol. 23) and by M. Tolmie in *The Triumph of the Saints*.

It is clear that the exercises of soul which led him to become an Independent eventually led him to become a Baptist — at a time when to be a Baptist meant scorn and persecution.

Happily at this time his marriage took place to a member of his own congregation, Hanna — "a suitable yoke fellow, who was with me in judgment." She was about 22 or 23 years old and was to be the partner of his joys and sorrows for almost 44 years.

CHAPTER 5

In Prison and Sickness

Quite early it was the will of his fellow-members that William Kiffin should preach or, to use the ancient terminology, ''improve amongst them the abilities God had given him.'' It seems that soon afterwards he was appointed the pastor. As this was a time when severe measures were used against nonconformists (the time of Archbishop Laud), the congregation had to meet early morning or late at night to escape persecution. Even so, often the meeting was disturbed.

One Lord's day, as he was leaving a meeting held in a house on Tower Hill, a few ruffians began to hurl stones at him. One hit him in the eye though mercifully he was not injured. Remarkably about a year later William Kiffin was asked to visit a poor man, a blacksmith, in Nightingale Lane. He turned out to be the ringleader of those who had caused the disturbance on Tower Hill. Now wasted away almost to a skeleton (Kiffin said his bones nearly came through his skin), he said he had been in perfect health at the time of the disturbance, but was taken ill immediately afterwards. It was his desire that William Kiffin should pray for him. Later the same day he died.

Not long after William Kiffin was seized at a meeting in Southwark and taken before the Justices of the Peace. The next day the Judge sent him to prison (the White Lion Prison) where he was kept for some time. Some of his fellow-prisoners had been guilty of daring robberies. Whilst there one of the prisoners developed a bitter hatred against him and also poisoned the minds of the other prisoners against him. This mysterious enemy resolved to stop at nothing and planned his murder. A number of the prisoners abruptly entered Kiffin's cell where he was enjoying a brief visit from his family. One had a great truncheon in his hand. However, they were so kindly welcomed that all their prejudices dissolved. Indeed, it was not long before Kiffin himself had to intervene to prevent the prisoners injuring the one who had stirred them up against him. Yet the bitter hatred still continued, and Kiffin was accused of speaking slanderous words against the King.

Later, in the providence of God, the Judge who had committed him to prison was himself impeached by Parliament and committed to the Tower of London. So eventually Kiffin was set free.

> "Thus it pleased God to deliver me out of the hands of malicious men, causing the rage of men to praise Him, and the remnant thereof He restrained."

Baptist historians and students of William Kiffin's life seem to have missed the fact that the sermon Kiffin preached before his arrest he later published. It was "printed for William Larner, at the Bible in Little-East-cheap, 1642," and bears the title *Certaine observations upon Hosea the second the 7th and 8th verses*. This is followed by a most interesting sub-title: "As they were delivered at a friends House who had broken his legg, for which meeting the author was committed to the White-Lyon by Sir Thomas Mallett late Judge of Assize for the County where he remained Prisoner of Jesus Christ."

The pamphlet (of over twenty pages) is dedicated to "The right worshipfill the Justices of peace for his Majesties County of Surrie." Kiffin tells us in this dedication that they had asked him why he should preach when he had not been to university nor had been ordained by the Bishops. His reply had been that he had a warrant from Scripture: "As every man hath received the gift, even so minister the same one to another, as good stewards of the manifold grace of God" (1 Peter 4.10). Also some of them had asked what he had said — which gave him the opportunity to publish the sermon and dedicate it to them. So his address at the end of the dedication is given as the "White Lyon" prison, where they had committed him.

In this preface he makes an interesting comment on his position:

> "Though I am accused and condemned for being at a conventicle, truly if praying for the King and Parliament and edifying one another in our most holy faith be keeping conventicles, then I am guilty. But if a conventicle be such a meeting as in the least measure is against any of these, then I detest it and abhor it."

This remained Kiffin's position for the rest of his life. He fought for liberty of conscience; but he was never a rebel, either against the King, Parliament or Cromwell. However, the great interest this pamphlet has for us is that it gives us the only idea we can ever have of Kiffin the preacher. What kind of preacher was he?

Well, this is an excellent sermon in true Puritan mould, with the usual divisions and uses. Indeed, had no name appeared we might easily have thought that it was preached by Flavel or Manton or one of the well-known Puritan divines. Perhaps one thing stands out. It is clear that the preacher is one who knows what it is to suffer for righteousness' sake. At the end he makes the following statement:

> "These being the observations and this the substance of all the matter which God was pleased to help me to deliver where I was apprehended, as I am publicly called by many to suffer for them, so I am not unwilling, being requested, to declare them to all, to such, and unto any it pleaseth God

24

by His good providence to dispose of them, desiring that all persons would 'try all things, and hold fast that which is good' (1 Thess. 5.21).''

A summary of the sermon appears at the end of this book.

William Kiffin was now about 25 years old: pastor of a church, engaged in secular employment, exposed to the insults of enemies of the truth — yet determined to obey God rather than men. Also, he had the care of a young family, and at this time few means to support them.

About this time he fell seriously ill and both his friends and his doctors gave him up. He was to all appearance a dying man.

In her great distress Kiffin's wife was prevailed on to go to see a Doctor Trigg. However, the doctor on seeing him pronounced his condition dangerous, and refused to have anything to do with it. At length, though, he was persuaded to have a try and God's blessing rested upon the treatment.

For three months Dr. Trigg cared for him, often coming twice a day. When asked about payment he would say, ''Leave it till he is well. I will have it all together.'' But this was a great burden to Kiffin and his wife. How could he pay? Sadly both his own and his wife's relations had concluded that, because of their religion, they would soon be ruined, and so kept money that should have belonged to them for themselves. They pacified their consciences by saying they would one day have to provide for the Kiffin children.

Remarkably Mrs. Kiffin noticed eminent people offer Dr. Trigg two golden sovereigns if he would visit one of their sick relatives; but he refused. And then he would slip off to see her husband.

At length when Kiffin was much restored, he plucked up courage to ask how much he owed. He had no money, and he did not feel it right to borrow. At last the doctor told him: ''A French crown'' — a mere trifle. Kiffin thought he was joking but, no, he would not have a penny more.

Dr. Trigg had been an utter stranger, and yet he said that he never tried harder to save a man's life — and with God's blessing he succeeded.

William Kiffin himself comments:

> ''This providence I looked upon to be very great to me at that time, and did wonderfully lead me to cleave unto the Lord in the discharge of my duty, that good word being made good: 'Trust in the Lord, and do good, and verily thou shalt be fed.'''

CHAPTER 6

"The Grand Ringleader of that Seduced Sect"

It seems difficult today to imagine the abuse which was heaped on the early Baptists. Some of this appears to have arisen from misunderstanding but there was a considerable degree of malice and bitterness. Above all the accusations were unjust. On the one hand the Baptists were accused of all manner of doctrinal error whilst on the other hand the most ridiculous suggestions were made concerning their practices — for instance, statements that they baptized women naked.

As a young minister who was beginning to take a leading part among the Baptists, William Kiffin had to bear more than his share of opprobrium.

On October 17th, 1642 (about the beginning of the Civil War) Kiffin and three other Baptists held a disputation in Southwark with Dr. Daniel Featley, a celebrated champion of the cause of infant baptism. Featley was at one time a member of the famous Westminster Assembly of Divines. All our information of what took place is found in a scurrilous work written by the doctor which went into six editions. It is entitled, *The Dippers dipt: or, the Anabaptists duck'd and plung'd over head and ears, at a Disputation in Southwark. Together with a large and full Discourse of the original, several sorts, peculiar errors, high attempts against the State, capital punishments, with an application to these times.* Dr. Featley loads his adversaries with plenty of abuse and relates some remarkable stories about them to prove them "1. an illiterate and sottish sect. 2. a lying and blasphemous sect. 3. an impure and carnal sect. 4. a cruel and bloody sect. 5. a profane and sacrilegious sect."

Throughout, Dr. Featley refers to William Kiffin contemptuously as "Cufin" or "this Cufin." We have no account from the Baptist side but it appears that the Baptists stood their ground courteously, though of course Featley claims the victory. The name "Anabaptists" was used by Kiffin's opponents, the word signifying "those who have been baptized again," most of those being baptized as believers having, of course, been already sprinkled as infants. But the word "Anabaptist" also had a forbidding aspect because there had been a group of fanatics at Munster who, in the previous century, had worked havoc, and *they* had been known as Anabaptists.

Featley dedicated his account of the disputation to the House of Lords claiming that the Anabaptists

> "preach and print and practise their heretical impieties openly; they hold their conventicles weekly in our chief cities and suburbs thereof...they flock in great multitudes to their Jordans, and both sexes enter into the river and are dipt.... And as they defile our rivers with their impure washings, and our pulpits with their false prophecies and fanatical enthusiasms, so the presses sweat and groan under the load of their blasphemies."

It was largely in response to such attacks that in 1644 the London Baptists issued a Confession of Faith. The clear Calvinism of this Confession and its moderate, scriptural terminology made it apparent to any unbiased mind that the Baptists were not fanatics, blasphemers, heretics, or any such thing; but that they were sober, law-abiding Christians who loved the doctrines of grace, commonly called Calvinism, and were more or less in agreement with their opponents on all vital matters, though differing on the *subjects* and the *manner* of baptism.

The Confession is entitled:

> "A Confession of Faith of seven congregations or churches of Christ in London, which are commonly but unjustly called Anabaptists."

This Confession did much to disarm antagonism and opposition from fair-minded people, and remained the established statement of Baptist belief till, being difficult to obtain, it was superseded by the Confession of 1689. It still abides, though, as a noble and gracious stand, soberly made, for the truth. Really England was amazed by the discovery of such moderation and orthodoxy, and even Daniel Featley could find little to which he could take exception!

The 1644 Confession was subscribed in the names of seven churches in London and, among others, signed by William Kiffin and Thomas Patience on behalf of the church at Devonshire Square. Kiffin was to be a signatory to every important Baptist document for the next fifty years or so. His wisdom, doctrinal understanding, firmness and moderation did much for the establishing of the churches and in contending against opposition. Later copies of the 1644 Confession were also signed by Hanserd Knollys, who with Kiffin was to take the lead during the next fifty years. Some eighteen years older than Kiffin, and a former clergyman, Hanserd Knollys was to live to the advanced age of 92, and the two were to remain friends, though differing in many ways.

Typical of the Calvinism of the Confession is:

> "Article 21. That Christ Jesus by His death did bring forth salvation and reconciliation only for the elect, which were those which God the Father gave Him; and that the gospel which is to be preached to all men as the ground of faith, is that Jesus is the Christ, the Son of the ever-blessed God, filled with the perfection of all heavenly and spiritual

29

excellencies, and that salvation is only and alone to be had through the believing in His Name.''

It was this belief in ''particular redemption'' which gave rise to the name ''Particular Baptists.''

There is also the clear statement on baptism — both the persons and the mode:

''Article 39. That baptism is an ordinance of the New Testament, given by Christ, to be dispensed only upon persons professing faith, or that are disciples, or taught, who upon a profession of faith, ought to be baptized.''

''Article 40. The way and manner of the dispensing of this ordinance the Scripture holds out to be dipping or plunging the whole body under water: it being a sign, must answer the thing signified, which are these: first, the washing the whole soul in the blood of Christ: secondly, that interest the saints have in the death, burial and resurrection; thirdly, together with a confirmation of our faith, that as certainly as the body is buried under water, and riseth again, so certainly shall the bodies of the saints be raised by the power of Christ, in the day of the resurrection, to reign with Christ.''

It has been supposed that the preface and conclusion were written by Kiffin. The conclusion ends:

''We confess that we know but in part, and that we are ignorant of many things which we desire and seek to know: and if any shall do us that friendly part to shew us, *from the Word of God*, that which we see not, we shall have cause to be thankful to God and them. But if any man shall impose upon us anything that we see not to be *commanded* by our Lord Jesus Christ, we should in His strength, rather embrace all reproaches and tortures of men, to be stripped of all outward comforts, and if it were possible to die a thousand deaths, rather than to do anything against the *least tittle of the truth of God*, or against the light of our own consciences. And if any shall call what we have said, *heresy*, then do we with the apostle acknowledge 'that after the way they call heresies so worship we the God of our Fathers'; disclaiming all heresies (rightly so called) because they are against Christ; and to be stedfast and immoveable, always abounding in *obedience* to Christ, as knowing our labour shall not be in vain in the Lord.''

(Some of the quotations are from the better known 1646 edition of this Confession.)

Soon afterwards, in 1645, *A Looking Glass for the Anabaptists* was published. In its title William Kiffin was mentioned by name as ''the author and grand ringleader of that seduced sect'' — so it is obvious that, at least among his opponents, he was regarded as the leading Baptist figure of the day. The full title reads:

''A Looking Glass for the Anabaptists, and the rest of the separatists: wherein they may clearly behold a brief confutation of a certain unlicensed, scandalous pamphlet, entitled, *The Remonstrance of the Anabaptists, by Way of Vindication of their Separation.* The impertinencies, incongruities, non-consequences, falsities and obstinacy of William Kiffin, the author and grand ringleader of that seduced sect is discovered and laid open to the view of every indifferent-eyed reader that will not shut his eyes against the truth. With certain queries, vindicated from Anabaptistical glosses, together with others propounded for the information and conviction, (if possible) reformation, of the said William Kiffin and his proselytes. By Josiah Ricraft, a well-willer to the truth.''

This was a curious tract of twenty-six pages written by a London Presbyterian merchant, who displayed much bigotry.

Yet another bitter opponent was a Presbyterian preacher, Thomas Edwards, whose *Gangraena* appeared about the same time. Edwards openly attacks Kiffin accusing him of many extravagances, and comparing him to a mountebank. As an example of his writing:

31

"Another of these fellows who counts himself inferior to none of the rest of his seduced brethren, one, whose name is Will. Kiffin, sometime servant to a brewer, (whose name is Lilburne, who was lately put into Newgate, upon occasion of scandalizing the Speaker of the honourable House of Commons), this man's man is now become a pretended preacher, and to that end hath by his enticing words, seduced and gathered a schismatical rabble of deluded children, servants and people without either parents' or masters' consent. (This truth is not unknown by some of a near relation to me, whose giddy-headed children and servants are his poor slavish proselytes.) For a further manifestation of him in a pamphlet called, *The Confession of Faith of the Seven Anabaptistical Churches*, there he is underwritten first, as metropolitan of that fraternity. I could relate, if time would permit, of somewhat I have had to do with him, in which he appeared to me to be a mountebank."

These were stirring times in both church and nation, but what Kiffin had to endure at least seems unchristian! Mercifully by showing Christian patience and forbearance, the Baptist cause was established. A letter sent by William Kiffin to Edwards is preserved:

"Sir,

You stand as one professing yourself to be instructed by Christ, with abilities from God to throw down error; and therefore to that end do preach every third day. May it therefore please you, and those that employ you in that work, to give them leave whom you so brand, as publicly to object against what you say, when your sermon is ended, as you declare yourself; and we hope it will be an increase of further light to all that fear God, and put a large advantage into your hands, if you have the truth on your side, to cause it to shine with more evidence, and I hope we shall do it with moderation as becometh Christians.

Your's,

1646   William Kiffin."

When we find Presbyterians so virulent in their condemnation of all who disagreed with them, we can begin to understand the well-known line from Milton's sonnet, written about this time:

"New presbyter is but old priest writ large."

CHAPTER 7

The Wealthy Merchant

It will be remembered that when William Kiffin was a boy, he had been dishonestly and unkindly treated by his relatives. Those who should have cared for him usurped everything for themselves. However, Kiffin was to prove that the God who had favoured him with His love and mercy was to favour him abundantly in providence. Not many of God's people, let alone His ministers, have known as much worldly prosperity as William Kiffin. God had a purpose in this which unfolded during the years of persecution that were to follow. His people were not only to find a faithful pastor in William Kiffin, but also a friend who was one of the wealthiest men in England. How we are reminded of the way in which God similarly used the wealth and generosity of John Thornton at the time of the Evangelical Revival!

When Kiffin left the service of the brewer where he was apprenticed with John Lilburne, he was left to himself. After working for a time as a glover he decided to trade as a merchant on his own account, and met with remarkable success. Not long before, the wool trade had fallen into decline, but now, setting out on business to Holland in 1643, William Kiffin prospered remarkably, and then, two years later, on a second venture, as the world would say "he made a fortune." Shortly before, despite his early success, he had feared lest he should be reduced to nothing.

On this second venture, William Kiffin took with him a young man from his congregation, apparently a man who was quite poor. Kiffin comments:

> "Although our stock was very little, it pleased God so to bless our endeavours that, from scores of pounds, He brought it to *many hundreds and thousands of pounds*, giving me more of this world than ever I could have thought to have enjoyed."

One thing that helped him in making so much money was the peculiar circumstances that prevailed during the war between England and Holland. The Dutch, with the help of Sweden and Denmark, had attempted to buy up all the pitch, tar, hemp and cordage that was available in Europe — things which the English fleet so badly required. Accordingly a Council of State order was proclaimed that if any merchants could obtain these valuable goods, then they would be given liberty to bring into the country other goods which were prohibited. Thus Kiffin was able to make great use of this newly-permitted freedom of trade, and amass great wealth through it. In this he proved once more the mysterious providence of God working for his good. He soon became known as one of the wealthiest wool merchants in the country.

This had blessed results. He was able to spend much time quietly at home in reading and meditating on the Word of God. Also, he was able to preach for his church without any salary and could in many, many ways be a help to the people of God in their need. Apart from the numerous ways in which he helped his persecuted brethren, in later years he was able to support at his own expense a Huguenot family which had fled from France to London following the Revocation of the Edict of Nantes.

"I was able," he says, "to give without receiving, which I bless the Lord He hath in some measure given me a heart to do."

During the Civil Wars it appears that William Kiffin also served as an officer in the Parliamentary army, though little is known concerning his involvement. (This is given as a fact by Holden Pike; on what authority we do not know.) After the execution of the King he is variously described as a Captain in the militia and later a Lieutenant-Colonel, and on one occasion was awarded £50 by Parliament, evidently for some military services.

One thing is clear: that he was still active in his enthusiasm for the truth. We find him engaged in "a famous disputation" with two General Baptists in Kent concerning the doctrines of grace and later engaged in a public dispute at Coventry on the subject of baptism. In the latter he was supported by Hanserd Knollys on the one hand and opposed by Obadiah Grew and John Bryan on the other. We are told that "it was managed with good temper and great moderation; both sides claimed the victory, and parted good friends. All granted that the Baptists came off with great reputation." About the same time we find Kiffin signing a *Declaration* published by Baptists and Congregationalists contending for religious liberty and supporting the work of magistrates as a divine appointment. It was made clear that they opposed polygamy, communism, and such things. The interesting thing is that they needed to do this. Again we find him opposing the Levellers.

Throughout his career Kiffin, though a champion of religious liberty, constantly opposed the extremes into which some of his friends were drawn. He was not a Fifth Monarchy man, he was not an enemy of Government; in fact, he was not really a politician in any sense, though he was to be unwillingly drawn into many of the great issues of the day. It is interesting to note that because of the esteem in which he was held, in 1647 Parliament appointed him assessor of taxes for Middlesex.

Also in September 1647, before the second Civil War, Kiffin met King Charles I, presumably negotiating for a promise of toleration. This was one of various approaches made at that time and the result was the preparation of a petition for a personal treaty with the King. A settlement arrived at by the Army (which contained many Particular Baptists) and King on the basis of toleration was well suited to remove from the Baptists the taint of being rebels, and so was attractive to Kiffin. Kiffin is thought to have opposed the King's execution, though a member of his church, Daniel Axtell was commander of the guard at the King's trial.

Again, we find that in 1648 the House of Commons "ordered that Mr. Kiffin and Mr. Knollys be permitted to preach in any part of Suffolk, at the petition of the Ipswich men." It is believed also that he became one of the Triers — godly men appointed to make sure that ministers in the established churches throughout the land were men of grace and ability.

In 1649 Kiffin appeared at the bar of the House of Commons to assure the House that the Particular Baptist churches did not support Lilburne's publication *The Second Part of England's New Chains Discovered*. He also returned thanks to God on their behalf "for affording to us the mercy of living peaceably without molestation, in the profession of godliness and honesty, under your authority and jurisdiction."

It is strange that we know so little about William Kiffin during the time of the Commonwealth and Oliver Cromwell's Protectorate. It is known that, if he did not always agree with Cromwell, he did not set himself up against him, and was reputed to be on good terms with him. His sentiments were that it is a Christian duty to be in subjection to the powers that be, whether the government be a monarchy or a republic. So in the Confession of Faith with which he had so much to do, drawn up whilst Charles I was still King, it is stated:

"The supreme magistracy of this kingdom we acknowledge to be king and parliament, now established,

37

freely chosen by the kingdom, and that we are to maintain and defend all civil laws and civil officers made by them, which are for the good of the commonwealth. And we acknowledge with thankfulness, that God hath made this present king and parliament honourable, in throwing down the prelatical hierarchy, because of their tyranny and oppression over us, under which this kingdom long groaned, for which we are ever engaged to bless God, and honour them for the same."

Kiffin seems more and more to have taken the lead among the Particular Baptist churches. So we find that when Obadiah Holmes was flogged in Boston, Massachussets, for baptizing a believer and an account was sent to London, Holmes addressed it: "Unto the well-beloved John Spilsbury and William Kiffin and to the rest in London." In particular he was vigilant to prevent any error creeping in. So we find him signing *Heartbleedings for Professors' Abominations* which was printed with later editions of the 1644 Confession. Especially this denounced those who "asserted that salvation by the cross of Christ was a mere history and shadow and that the Scriptures are but a letter." In reply to charges of being uncharitable, the pamphlet insisted that "true love and charity is not the soothing of any in their sins." Again we find him in 1653 corresponding with the churches in Ireland and Wales, encouraging and restraining them and also travelling about to give the churches help and advice in their various problems. This was to continue for many years. His services in encouraging the brethren in Ireland to be submissive to the civil magistrates were acknowledged by Henry Cromwell, the Protector's son.

Yet on Thursday, July 12th, 1655, he was summoned before the Lord Mayor at the Guildhall. His offence? Preaching "that the baptism of infants was unlawful." Mercifully, he was treated with respect by the Lord Mayor — for an ordinance passed some years before demanded severe penalties for such ''heresy.'' The Lord Mayor said he was busy and would defer the execution of the penalty demanded by the Act till the following Monday morning. Kiffin never heard any more of the matter.

Amidst all this we find William Kiffin sitting as a Member of Parliament for Middlesex from 1656 to 1658.

One thing does seem sad. We have so much information about so many interesting details in Kiffin's life but little or nothing about the preaching of the gospel and its gracious effect — the most important thing of all. And we believe Kiffin knew this, and felt it. Amidst all these other things, the honour of God and the blessing of His people was uppermost.

Yet we do know that these were years of growth and blessing, though so trying, and we are delighted to have this account (from 1656) of what was happening in the churches:

''We have seen the Lord exalted and His train filling the temple. We have in some measure been embracing our dear Jesus who hath made us even sick with love and overcome with longings for that day of glory when we shall appear with Him and be made like Him and shall for ever be with Him not only beholding but enjoying glory. O, if the crumbs be so sweet as to make us rejoice with joy unspeakable and full of glory, what will it be when faith and hope will stand aside and we sit down at table to enjoy fulness of glory.''

CHAPTER 8

Rebellion, Treason, Forgery, Imprisonment

The death of the Lord Protector, Oliver Cromwell, on September 3rd, 1658, was bound to bring changes. Soon the monarchy was to be restored and, under that licentious King, Charles II, an era of bitter persecution for the nonconformists was to begin. It was very unlikely that such a leading figure as William Kiffin would escape, especially because, in addition to his eminence as a minister, his position as a leading merchant and a man of wealth laid him bare to the jealousy of his enemies.

It was even before the return of Charles II to England that Kiffin was seized — even though he had sought to live peaceably throughout the Protectorate. General Monk (who had been one of Cromwell's supporters, but now was to take a leading part in the return of King Charles II) took up his quarters near Kiffin's house. Suddenly, a few days later, at midnight, some of his soldiers seized Kiffin and carried him to the guard house at St. Paul's. Rumour spread round the city that a great quantity of arms had been found in his house — with, of course, all kinds of suspicions about what he had intended to do.

A letter was immediately sent to the Lord Mayor concerning the scandal brought upon him (and others who were also seized). It was explained that what few arms were in his house were only what it was normal to have. (What dangerous days these were when it was taken for granted that ordinary people needed to be armed!) Happily the Lord Mayor quickly dealt with the matter. Kiffin and the others were released — and their arms restored to them. The letter was published with the note: "A Letter to the Lord Mayor by Lieut.-Col. Kiffin."

About this time Venner's rebellion took place. Thomas Venner preached at a small meeting house in Coleman Street, London, where he enthused his hearers with expectations of a fifth universal monarchy on earth, soon to take place under the personal reign of Jesus. About fifty of his hearers marched out of the meeting house, well armed, with a desire to overturn the government. Assembling in St. Paul's churchyard they killed a man who when challenged answered, "For God and the King." Trained bands were sent out but proved unable to master them so the regular soldiers had to be called out. After a fierce encounter Venner's supporters were either killed, captured or scattered, Venner himself later being hanged. Thomas Venner was not a Baptist, but some Baptists had "Fifth Monarchy" sympathies, and the occasion was used by the authorities to renew persecution of nonconformists. William Kiffin was no Fifth Monarchy man and took the opportunity to make clear that neither he nor his congregation had any sympathy at all with the rebellion. He signed a protestation expressing the abhorrence of the Baptists of what they call "the late wicked and most horrible treasonable insurrection and rebellion in the city of London"; and declared their loyalty to the King.

About the same time Kiffin was abused in a vicious squib entitled "The life and approaching death of William Kiffin." Typical of it is the following extract:

"After two or three conferences with Patience (Patient) and the devil, he was by instinct and revelation appointed to the work, and ordained Musty of all heretics and sectaries. But this was not without great heartburnings of other gifted brethren, who upon his assumption to the Pontificacy and Primacy began to separate and divide from the congregation, and to set up for themselves in their particular conventicles, intending to weaken Kiffin's design and party; but the wenches stuck close unto him, and he prevailed, as we see unto this day."

Also this scurrilous writer declares:

"If you compare his speeches in that mock parliament with his excercises and lectures at his bedlam, you would wonder that one and the same man could be so silent and clamorous; but he was Will the whisperer to the one and the bawler to the other."

(Remarkable description of a Particular Baptist meeting: "*bedlam*"!)

For a time there was quiet. But then a most strange and unwarranted attack was made on Kiffin. On December 24th, 1660, the Princess of Orange died. She was the King's sister and the mother of William III. She was only twenty-nine. Following the Princess's death a cruel plot was laid against Kiffin — which could have cost him his life.

A letter was forged, supposedly written to Kiffin from Taunton. The substance of it was (in Kiffin's own words):

"That the Princess of Orange being now dead, they were now ready to put their design into execution; if, according to my promise, I would provide and send down powder, matches, bullets, etc."

At midnight on the Saturday Kiffin was arrested and taken to the guard house at Whitehall. All day Sunday he was kept there, being threatened and scoffed at by the soldiers. Next day he had to appear before General Monk and some of the Privy Council. The letter was read and he was accused of being guilty.

Protesting his innocence, William Kiffin spoke of his utter abhorrence of such a thing. He said he had never heard of the man by whom the letter was written. After this he was shut away and strictly guarded. "Under this dispensation," he says, "I found much support from God, and, knowing my innocence, I did not doubt but He would in some way or other work deliverance for me."

Next day he was taken before the Lord Chief Justice. As it was observed that the coach in which he was being taken was guarded on each side by soldiers, a great crowd gathered out of curiosity, and there were cries of "Traitors!" "Rogues!" "Hang them!"

Being given liberty to speak freely before the Lord Chief Justice, Kiffin was able to prove that the letter was forged. First, the plot was supposed to begin after the Princess's death yet the letter was dated three days before she died. Second, even if there was a mistake in the date, it was impossible for a letter to have been written from London to Taunton and a reply received again in London in the short interval between the Princess's death and Kiffin's arrest.

And God did appear for William Kiffin. The Lord Chief Justice told him he was sure he was innocent, and if the writer of the forged letter could be found, he would be dealt with. "Thus," says Kiffin, "did God work deliverance for me, and ensnared those who contrived the letter in the work of their own hands; and we, having escaped as a bird out of the snare of the fowler, had great cause to praise His holy name."

It seems almost unbelievable that an honourable Christian minister should have to endure such things as these.

But the time soon arrived when most bitter persecution of the nonconformists broke loose; and very shortly after this Kiffin and some of his friends were imprisoned for meeting illegally for worship. The meeting was on the Lord's day in Shoreditch when they were seized and sent to (what Kiffin calls) "the new prison." However, after three or four days they were set free.

After this there was a little respite. But in the mysterious providence of God something entirely different took place · — which might have ruined him, yet instead wonderfully gave him a high and honourable standing in the sight of the King and his ministers.

CHAPTER 9

Adviser to the King

At this time a trading company known as the Hamburgh Company prevailed with the King to give them the monopoly of exporting woollen goods to Holland and Germany. This, of course, caused much anger among the other woollen merchants, and those in the West of England protested to their Members of Parliament. Interestingly, they named William Kiffin as the man who could give most information and an honest opinion on the matter.

So Kiffin found himself before a Committee of the House of Commons at its own request, and gave what information he could. After several debates the House besought the King to annul his royal proclamation. First, however, the King wished it to be discussed in the Privy Council, and asked William Kiffin to be present. How mysterious the vicissitudes in this good man's life: one time accused of treason, another time personally requested by the King to aid the Privy Council!

Several leading men of the Hamburgh Company boasted that before long they would have Kiffin in the Gatehouse Prison. "But," says Kiffin, "though man thought evil against me, God overruled it for good."

Kiffin simply and ably gave his reasons why the granting of the monopoly of exporting woollen goods was not for the good of England or England's prosperity. Several Members of Parliament immediately expressed their agreement, pointing out that many woollen merchants and clothiers would be severely injured.

Again a meeting of the Privy Council was called, and

again the King desired Kiffin to be there. This time the members of the Hamburgh Company began to assail Kiffin's character, speaking of many things he was supposed to have said and done. Humbly Kiffin replied (his own words):

> "That in the late times I had concerned myself only in my own calling, not having advanced my estate either by public titles or public places, and that what I had now offered to his Majesty and his most honourable Council was in obedience to his Majesty's commands, being those sentiments which I thought were for the good and advantage of the kingdom. But if his Majesty thought otherwise, I desired humbly to submit to his Majesty's great wisdom therein."

The result was that the King recalled his proclamation and withdrew the monopoly. But much more than this. Both the King and the Privy Council took a liking to Kiffin. How the Scripture was fulfilled: "When a man's ways please the Lord, He maketh even his enemies to be at peace with him"! Lord Arlington (at one time Secretary of State and Lord Chamberlain), an enemy of God and godliness, later told Kiffin that whenever accusations were made, or lists of supposedly disaffected persons were presented to the King, he would never believe anything said against William Kiffin. (We are reminded of how in a similar way Henry VIII took a liking to Latimer.) Also, the Earl of Clarendon, the Lord Chancellor, Charles II's chief adviser, became "very much my friend."

One of the most interesting events in the life of William Kiffin concerns his close connection with the King. Charles II was always short of money. On one occasion he sent for Kiffin. "Can you lend me £40,000?" he said. (How many millions would £40,000 be today?)

Kiffin thought quickly. He knew that though it was only a loan, he would never see the money again. Yet how could he refuse? Then he replied he would not *lend* money to the King, but would his Majesty accept a free gift of £10,000? The King was only too glad to receive it. Kiffin often said that in this way he had saved himself the sum of £30,000!

In the providence of God, Kiffin's friendship with the King was put to good account, especially in the way he was able to help the persecuted people of God. These were persecuting times. In 1662 about 2,000 ministers had been evicted from the Church of England for refusing to conform to every detail in the prayer book. The Conventicle Act forbade the meeting of nonconformists for worship. But now in 1664 persecution reached the height of madness when a few humble Baptists at Aylesbury were sentenced to death for meeting together — an old law from Queen Elizabeth's reign being invoked.

Twelve people, ten men and two women, had been seized at a Baptist meeting at Aylesbury in Buckinghamshire. Having been legally convicted, three months later they were required either to conform to the Church of England or leave the country or, failing either of these, be put to death. Nobly the little group refused either to conform or leave the country. Whereupon sentence of death was passed on them, and they were sent back to prison to await their execution. To their honour we record their names (as far as known): Stephen Dagnal, minister; ---- Ellit, a teacher; William Whitchurch, a glover, and deacon in their congregation; Thomas Hill, a linen draper; William Welch, a tallow chandler; Thomas Monk, a farmer; ---- Brandon, a shoemaker; three other men, whose names are not known; Ann Turner, spinster; and Mary Jackman, a widow with six children.

The sentence was no sooner passed than their houses were raided and their goods seized. One of the condemned persons, Brandon the shoemaker, was so overcome by the tears and entreaties of his wife that he recanted. Who cannot but feel sympathy for him? He needed only to go to the parish church, where possibly the truth was preached in the letter. However, the good man endured such horror of soul that it exceeded all his fear either of death or for his family. In deep repentance he gave himself up and voluntarily returned to prison, resolving to die with his friends for the truth's sake.

Meantime, the son of Thomas Monk (one of the condemned ones) immediately on the passing of the sentence had taken horse and galloped as quickly as possible to London. Seeking out William Kiffin he gave him details of the sad story, and Kiffin hastened to Lord Chancellor Hyde who then laid their case before King Charles II. The King seemed most surprised that anyone could still be put to death for his religion, but when told of the ancient Act that was being used, he promised a pardon and gave orders to that effect to the Lord Chancellor. But then, realising that those who had hastily passed the death sentence might just as hastily put it into force, the King kindly granted an immediate royal reprieve.

This being passed over to Thomas Monk, he then made all possible haste back to Aylesbury and produced the royal pardon. The Baptists' cruel persecutors were amazed that such a thing could have taken place, whilst the twelve prisoners were overwhelmed with joy.

But the King certainly wished to remain on friendly terms with a man who could make him a present of £10,000.

CHAPTER 10

Mysterious Accusations

It was William Kiffin's contemporary, John Bunyan, who wrote:

"A Christian man is never long at ease;
When one fright's gone, another doth him seize."

And so Kiffin proved it. True, he had the favour of both the King and the Lord Chancellor. But ungodly men did not like his religion, and the fact of his wonderful prosperity (in 1671-2 we find him Master of the Leathersellers' Company, one of the City of London Guilds), and now his influence at court, could not but provoke jealousy. And jealousy has always been "cruel as the grave."

Of all things, William Kiffin was now accused of plotting to murder the King! This time he says, "My enemies aimed at nothing less than my life." It was midnight, and he was seized by order of no less a person than the Duke of Buckingham and taken under the guard of soldiers to York House. The Duke himself accused him, saying, "You would have hired two men to kill the King. You told them if they would not do it, you would do it yourself. Confess! Then care will be taken that you do not suffer." Apparently one A. Bradley had given the information: "Lieutenant-Colonel Kiffin said that the Scarlet Whore, the King, must be stabbed, and it could be done easily in his night clothes." Also, he was accused of stating he could command seven hundred men in the rebellion.

Kiffin was astounded. Protesting his innocence he

said, "I thank God that I abhor from my soul such a design against the meanest man in the kingdom, much more towards his Majesty."

But Buckingham would not listen. He said he knew it could be proved. He would bring two witnesses. Meantime he must remain under guard.

This was trouble; and though innocent, Kiffin was not without his fears.

> "But," he says, "it pleased the Lord, whose care and goodness had been extended towards me in all difficulties to that day, greatly to revive me, bringing that scripture with great power upon my soul: 'Fear thou not; for I am with thee: be not dismayed; for I am thy God: I will strengthen thee; yea, I will help thee; yea, I will uphold thee with the right hand of My righteousness.' I was now so greatly quieted in my own heart that my fears vanished, and I was made willing to submit to whatever the pleasure of God should be towards me in this matter."

Later, after examination, he was kept prisoner but, being visited by Lady Ranelagh (seemingly a godly nonconformist herself), she advised him to write to the Lord Chancellor, and delivered the letter herself. The letter was read before the King in council, who enquired if there was any charge against Kiffin. An order was immediately passed for him to be set free. Thus he proved God's faithfulness to His own promise.

Yet this was not quite the end. With a heart full of gratitude next morning Kiffin went to thank the Lord Chancellor personally. Whilst waiting to see him, he noticed a number of dignitaries go in and was then called to meet them. They were amazed he was not still a prisoner. The Lord Chancellor told him that he knew the King had ordered his freedom, but just after the Duke of Buckingham had come in with his accusations. So he must return to prison again. Yet once more the King kindly gave him his freedom.

Kiffin comments:

> "This great deliverance was a cause for wonder to all that heard of it; for many who were taken at the same time, whose charges were not by any means so high as mine, were kept in the Gatehouse more than six months. Thus did the Lord work deliverance by His own hand."

Yet his enemies were still determined to secure his downfall. The next trial was when he was sent for by Judge Sir Richard Brown. He began to be plied with strange questions. Where had he been that summer? What had he been doing? Was it not true that he had persuaded his church and congregation to enter into a league against the government?

Kiffin replied. Most of the time he had been in London. Sometimes he had visited a relative in Hertfordshire. His church and congregation only met together for the good of their souls. They were not concerned with politics.

"Ah!" said the judge, "there was someone there who will bear witness to it." But then he sent Kiffin home — and no more was heard of the matter.

However, at long last Kiffin's enemies thought they had succeeded. One evening at about six o'clock a party of soldiers burst into his house, and began a thorough search. They were sure they could find incriminating evidence. All his papers were ransacked — but nothing could be found.

But at last they found what they wanted — or so they thought! Searching beneath the desk of Kiffin's secretary, there it was: a book carefully hidden away. Quickly snatching it, they cried out one to another that they had found something. But to their dismay it was only a little book entitled *Reynard the Fox*. Apparently the secretary read it in his spare time but kept it where his master could not find it.

After the Reynard the Fox affair there was peace at last

— for the present. Though Kiffin had to appear before the chief commander, he was set free on condition he would always be ready to be questioned if required.

"After this," he says, "I was suffered to remain in my habitation in peace, enjoying the comforts of my relations, and what it hath pleased God to give me."

Some of these deliverances he recorded are nothing short of astonishing. How could a godly nonconformist expect any favours from the ungodly crowd who surrounded Charles II? But they must have had a powerful conviction continually of his integrity. It was a time of dreadful persecution, many ministers being stripped of their liberty and their possessions; but here was William Kiffin, still free, and still preaching to his own congregation. Not only so but he was even able to obtain licences for others to preach.

CHAPTER 11

Personal Sorrows

But now there were troubles of a different sort. Not only did the persecuting spirit against nonconformists become more severe, causing incredible hardship, but now William Kiffin began to taste the cup of personal sorrow.

His eldest son, also William, died on August 31st, 1669, aged only 20. His father felt this blow very keenly, as William was such a loving son, and also a godly boy. It was a time when he needed to prove the reality of his religion, and he wrote:

> "It pleased God to take out of the world to Himself my eldest son, which was no small affliction to me and my dear wife. His obedience to his parents, and forwardness in the ways of God, were so conspicuous as to make him very amiable in the eyes of all who knew him. The grief I felt for his loss did greatly press me down with more than ordinary sorrow; but in the midst of my great distress it pleased the Lord to support me by that blessed word being brought powerfully to my mind: 'Is thine eye evil because I am good? Is it not lawful for Me to do what I will with Mine own?' These words did quiet my heart so that I felt a perfect submission to His sovereign will, being well satisfied that it was for the great advantage of my dear son, and a voice to me to be more humble and watchful over my own ways."

Thus we get a glimpse right into William Kiffin's heart. His son lies buried along with his father in Bunhill Fields.

His second son he lost shortly afterwards in peculiar circumstances. (How many *unusual* things we meet with in

Kiffin's life!) This son, who was not very well, had a desire to travel abroad; so he set sail for Italy on board a ship whose captain was known to Kiffin. Because of his fears of Roman Catholicism and its corrupting influence, Kiffin arranged for a young minister to go as a companion. Irresponsibly, however, the minister left young Kiffin and the ship at Leghorn and journeyed to Rome.

On his way back home Kiffin's son had to pass through Venice. Being a true son of his father he was not backward in speaking about true religion — even to a priest with whom he came into contact. He never did return home. *The wicked priest poisoned him.*

Kiffin's only comment about the young minister who failed him so solemnly is: ''I pray God that this sin may not be laid to his charge.''

Not long after he also lost a loved daughter, Priscilla.

Amidst all the changes, persecutions, imprisonments, accusations and now bereavements, William Kiffin had always had the wonderful favour of a loving, loyal, gracious wife. Whatever trials there were abroad, she was always there to encourage and comfort him at home. Now the time came for him to lose her (October 5th, 1682, aged 67). Her husband writes:

> ''It pleased the Lord to take to Himself my dear and faithful wife, with whom I had lived nearly forty-four years, whose tenderness to me and faithfulness to God were such as cannot by me be expressed, as she constantly sympathised with me in all my afflictions.''

He then bears this witness:

> ''I can truly say I never heard her utter the least discontent under all the various providences that attended either me or her. She eyed the hand of God in all our sorrows so as constantly to encourage me in the ways of God. Her death was the greatest sorrow to me that ever I met with in the world.''

Against this sad background he was twice prosecuted for "conventicle keeping" (meeting for worship other than in the Church of England). Many malicious "informers" were after him as, on account of his great wealth, they hoped to make some gain themselves. Through technical flaws in the proceedings he was able to go free. On one occasion £300 would have been the penalty.

At the time of the Rye House plot to assassinate the King, Kiffin's house was searched on suspicion of his taking part in it. His son-in-law, Joseph Hayes, a banker, was brought for trial accused of sending money to Sir Thomas Armstrong (who was later beheaded for his part in the plot, and his head set up on the city gates). Hayes himself narrowly escaped with his life.

Whilst trying to help his son-in-law, Kiffin found one night a packet of letters left for him. Who had brought them no one could tell. One was addressed to Lord Justice Jeffreys; the other, full of treasonable words, to Kiffin. Kiffin immediately forwarded them to the Lord Chief Justice — and remarkably never heard any more about them. "Thus this storm also blew over."

"The wise providence of God," wrote Kiffin, "who orders all things as He pleaseth, reserved farther trials to attend me in my old age; yet, through His goodness, He hath been pleased to give me some measure of strength to bear me up under them all: and in the sharpest of which I have seen goodness and mercy following me."

CHAPTER 12

The Greatest Trial

But now was to come the greatest trial of William Kiffin's life — the cruel death of two of his beloved grandsons. Their father, Benjamin Hewling, had died and Kiffin had taken charge of the family, helping to give the two boys, Benjamin and William, an excellent education. He treated them as his own sons.

The story of the rebellion of the Duke of Monmouth, illegitimate son of Charles II, soon after the succession to the throne of the Roman Catholic James II is well known. Many godly people down in the west country supported Monmouth, believing him to be the rightful heir to the throne, and also badly wanting a Protestant as King.

Terrible were the recriminations when the ill-trained army, sometimes fighting only with spades and pitchforks, was defeated. In the cruel Judge Jeffreys there was one ready to hasten them through the mockery of a trial to their execution.

Among those who were thus put to death were the two Hewling boys. When the Duke of Monmouth sailed to England, William was being educated in Holland. He accompanied the Duke. Benjamin, having talked with those who dreaded popery, furnished himself with arms, and went to join the Duke.

After the disastrous defeat at Sedgemoor, the two brothers attempted to escape by sea, but contrary winds drove their ship back to England. Compelled to land, they were soon taken prisoner. After a short stay in Exeter jail they were sent to Newgate in London, and after three weeks back to the west for trial.

Their venerable grandfather did all he could to save them, even agreeing to pay the large sum of £3,000 if they were set free. But Judge Jeffreys was so determined that very few of the prisoners escaped.

The Hewlings' sister, Hannah, was untiring in her efforts for her brothers' deliverance. She even managed to gain an audience with the King himself to plead on their behalf. The story is told of how she was introduced into the King's presence by John Churchill (later the famous Duke of Marlborough). While they waited in the ante-room Churchill kindly assured the young lady of his most hearty wishes for her success. "But," he said, "I dare not flatter you with any hope." Pointing to an object made out of marble, he added, "That marble is as capable of feeling compassion as the King!"

So it proved. The Hewlings were executed — William at Lyme (now, Lyme Regis) on September 12th, 1685, and Benjamin at Taunton on September 30th.

The last days of the two young men, noted alike for their handsome appearance and their godliness, made a great impression.

On August 30th both of them told their sister how they were proving the grace and goodness of God in their sufferings, supporting and strengthening them. In Newgate they had been badly treated and had travelled west loaded with heavy irons and inhumanly dealt with. Yet they confessed they had never been happier. Why? Because they had a sweet sense of the love of Christ in their hearts, being blessed with the knowledge of pardoned sin, and feeling they could leave everything in the hand of a wise and gracious God.

"Anything what pleaseth God," they said. "What He sees best, so be it. We know He is able to deliver, but if not, blessed be His name. Death is not terrible now, but desirable.''

On September 6th Benjamin was ordered to Taunton to be tried there. To his sister, in saying farewell, he said, ''O blessed be God for afflictions! I would not have been without them for all the world.''

William was kept at Dorchester where his sister could still visit him. He spoke with much admiration of the grace of God which had called him from death to life. He went right back in his thoughts to when he was in Holland and in secret the Holy Spirit whispered in his heart, ''Seek ye My face.'' He was then shown the evil of sin and the vital necessity of Christ, being brought feelingly to cling to Him for justification and eternal life. In Christ he had found joy and comfort beyond anything on earth.

The following evening he received news he was to die the next day, and should be taken to Lyme. He felt that God had chosen best for him. He said:

> ''He knows what the temptations of life might have been. I might have lived and forgotten God, but now I am going where I shall sin no more. O, it is a blessed thing to be freed from sin and to be with Christ. O! the riches of the love of God in Christ to sinners. O! how great were the sufferings of Christ for me; beyond all I can undergo! How great is that glory to which I am going! It will soon swallow up all our sufferings here.''

As he was taken prisoner along the road from Dorchester to Lyme, multitudes with sorrow witnessed his journey. To all he spoke most graciously of the glory to which they were going. Passing through beautiful country, he said:

> ''This is a glorious creation; but what then is the paradise of God to which we are going? It is but a few hours and we shall be there and be for ever with the Lord.''

Just before his execution, reading John 14.18 to one of his fellow-sufferers, he said,

"Here is a sweet promise for us: 'I will not leave you comfortless; I will come unto you.' Christ will be with us to the last."

And to one who said goodbye to him,

"Farewell till we meet in heaven. Presently I shall be with Christ. O I would not change conditions with anyone in this world. I would not stay behind for ten thousand worlds."

His end is beautifully recorded by his sorrowing sister:

"Afterwards he prayed for about three-quarters of an hour with the greatest fervency, exceedingly blessing God for Jesus Christ; adoring the riches of His grace in him, for all the glorious fruits of it towards him, praying for the peace of the church of God and of these nations in particular; all with such eminent assistance of the Spirit of God as convinced, astonished and melted into pity the hearts of all present, even the most malicious adversaries, forcing tears and expressions of regret from them; some saying they knew not what would become of them after death, but it was evident he was going to great happiness.

"When he was just departing out of the world, with a joyful countenance he said, 'O now my joy and comfort is that I have a Christ to go to,' and so sweetly resigned his spirit to Christ."

His body being permitted by the sheriff to be buried, he was laid in the grave in Lyme churchyard, September 13th, 1685.

Meanwhile Benjamin had been brought to Taunton. When his sister arrived to visit him, he said:

"We have no cause to fear death if the presence of God be with us. There is no evil in it, the sting being taken away. It is nothing but our ignorance of the glory that the saints pass into by death which makes it appear dark to ourselves or our relations. If we be in Christ, what is this world that we should desire an abode in it? It is all vain and unsatisfying; full of sin and misery."

He had heard of his brother's death and cheerfully spoke of expecting soon to follow himself. He testified that his lonely time in Newgate prison was the sweetest in his whole life.

At first a report came that there were to be no more executions; but soon this was proved false, and late at night on September 29th news came that he must die next morning. This was quite a shock. Yet he said, "Though men design to surprise, God doth and will perform His Word, to be a very present help in time of trouble."

Next morning, writes his sister:

> "When I saw him again his cheerfulness and comfort were much increased: waiting for the sheriff with the greatest sweetness and serenity of mind.... With a smiling countenance he discoursed of the glory of heaven.... His hope and comfort still increasing with the assurance of an interest in that glorious inheritance to the possession of which he was now going. He said, 'Death was more desirable than life, and he would rather die than live any longer here....' Then reading the Scriptures and musing with himself he intimated the great comfort which God conveyed to his soul in it, saying, 'O what an invaluable treasure is this blessed Word of God! In all conditions here is a store of strong consolation.' One desiring his Bible, he said, 'No, this shall be my companion to the last moment of my life.'"

Soon he and the others were mercilessly hurried away by the sheriff, scarcely being permitted to take leave of their friends. His sister has solemnly recorded his last moments:

> "When they came to the place of execution, which was surrounded with spectators, many who waited their coming with great sorrow said, that when they saw him and them come with such cheerfulness and joy and evidence of the presence of God with them, it made death appear with another aspect. They first embraced each other with the greatest affection; then two of the elder persons praying

audibly they joined with great seriousness. Then he desired leave of the sheriff to pray particularly; but he would not grant it, and only asked him if he would pray for the King? He answered, 'I pray for all men.' He then requested that they might sing a psalm. The sheriff told them it must be with the rope round their necks; which they cheerfully accepted, and sang with such heavenly joy and sweetness that many who were present said it both broke and rejoiced their hearts. Thus in the experience of the delightfulness of praising God on earth, he willingly closed his eyes on a vain world to pass to that eternal employment.''

Such awful yet glorious happenings remind us of the martyrdoms in the reign of Queen Mary and of the covenanters in Scotland. How the Lord has in all ages proved His ability to support His people in the face of death! Over three hundred people were put to death by Judge Jeffreys at that time.

It is obvious how all this must have been a painful trial to their old grandfather. Benjamin was only 22 years old, William 19. In fact, Jeffreys at the trial of one of the brothers had cried out, ''Your grandfather deserves to suffer death as well as you!''

William Kiffin later wrote:

''It was a great comfort to me, and still is, to observe what testimony they left behind them of that blessed interest they had in the Lord Jesus and holy confidence of their eternal happiness.''

The question may be asked: were the Hewling boys justified in taking part in the rebellion? Well, hundreds of godly people felt they were fighting for a righteous cause — the overthrow of popery — and almost regarded the rebellion as a crusade. In fact, it has been wisely commented that the Glorious Revolution only three years later was a similar rebellion — yet, having this time succeeded, it has been as much honoured as Monmouth's rebellion has been condemned.

The well-known minister, Benjamin Keach, wrote a lamentation for the Hewling brothers in his *Distressed Zion Relieved,* dedicated to King William and Queen Mary. He ends:

> "What cruel tyrants had we lately here,
> That two such tender branches would not spare?
> But when I think of grace that they had store,
> And with what patience they their sufferings bore,
> It gives such comfort I can weep no more.
> What testimony did they leave behind,
> Of that sweet joy which they in Christ did find?
> When wicked men all pity did deny,
> Our Saviour to compassion's moved thereby;
> And doubtless they are placed in that high sphere
> Where the spirits of just men triumphant are."

No doubt it will be asked, "What happened to the Hewlings' sister, who endured so much and displayed such bravery?" The next year she was married to Henry Cromwell, the Lord Protector's grandson, thus uniting the families of those two eminent men, William Kiffin and Oliver Cromwell. Her own persecuted family and the Cromwells she sought to shield in every possible way. She died, aged 79, on March 27th, 1732.

The descendants of Oliver Cromwell who are alive today are descended from this brave woman, Kiffin's granddaughter, and so from William Kiffin himself.

CHAPTER 13

Alderman of the City

With the coming of James II to the throne nothing but trouble could be expected by the nonconformists. Charles II was secretly a Roman Catholic but his brother did not hesitate openly to avow himself one. However, so keen was the King to promote the interests of the Romanists that he abolished all penal laws against dissenters — i.e. all those who would not conform to the national church. Of course, this embraced two extremes: Roman Catholics on the one hand, Independents, Presbyterians and Baptists on the other.

A few ministers were thrilled to find that freedom of worship was at last permitted, but with the great majority the love of the truth prevailed, and nobly they refused to express gratitude for this new freedom. They knew the motive and, as Kiffin commented, that there was a sting in the tail.

"A new project was set on foot to engage the Protestant dissenters in that measure by giving them the liberty of their meetings, and promising them equal authority in the nation with others; but this was in the tail of it, to engage them thereby to promote the taking off the tests, and to strengthen the Popish interest by setting the Protestant dissenters against the Protestants of the Church of England."

Kiffin did all that he could to persuade nonconformists to realise what lay behind this new toleration. He was a true Protestant who put the truth of God before personal interest. Later Kiffin's hand was the first to sign a document which declares: "It being our professed judgment, and we on all occasions shall manifest the same, to venture our all for the Protestant religion, and the liberties of our native country.''

Remarkably William Kiffin knew James II well personally just as he had known Charles II. The King badly wanted the support of this man, so widely respected and revered, who had so much wealth on the one hand and so much influence among the nonconformists on the other.

So when the King disenfranchised the City of London he personally appointed Kiffin to be an alderman. An affecting story is told of the interview — which reveals much of the character of both men. James II sent for Kiffin to attend at court. On his arrival he found many lords and gentlemen gathered together. But the King approached Kiffin and tried to talk to him as graciously (in a worldly sense) as he could. He spoke of his favour towards the nonconformists and told Kiffin he had nominated him as an alderman under his new charter.

''Sire,'' replied Kiffin, ''I am a very old man'' (he was now over 70) ''and have withdrawn myself from all kinds of business for some years past, and am incapable of doing any service in such an affair to your Majesty in the city. Besides, Sire'' — and here, with tears streaming down his face, Kiffin fixed his eyes steadfastly on the King — ''the death of my grandsons gave a wound to my heart which is still bleeding, and never will close but in the grave.''

This seems to be one of the few occasions when anything really affected King James II. He was deeply struck by the manner, the freedom and the spirit of this unexpected rebuke. Total silence ensued. The King seemed to shrink from the horrid event of which he had been reminded. A minute or two passed; then he recovered himself.

"Mr. Kiffin," he said, "I shall find a balsam for that sore," and immediately turned away to speak to a lord in waiting.

William Kiffin used all the means he could to be excused from being an alderman. There were so many difficulties. But it was made plain that the King badly wanted him — for his own ends. Those in authority told him clearly that it was in vain he refused; also there would be many honours and advantages for him personally. ''But I thank the Lord,'' says Kiffin, ''those proffers were no snare to me. Being fully possessed in my judgment that the design was the total ruin of the Protestant religion, which I hope I can say was and is dearer to me than my life, I remained without accepting the office.''

As time went on it became clear that Kiffin was running great hazards in refusing the King. The Lord Mayor said he should be sent to Newgate prison, whilst a leading judge advised him that he could be fined thousands of pounds.

So in the end, out of necessity, he accepted, though at first he did not attend.

We pause and think what a remarkable change had taken place with passing years. The young penniless apprentice, friendless and running away, now (nearly 60 years later) personally appointed alderman by the King in the very same city.

At length Kiffin agreed to attend the Lord Mayor's Day dinner when the King was invited, and paid his £50 to help defray the charge, and the next day took his place as an alderman. On attending the dinner to his annoyance William Kiffin found that the Pope's nuncio, Cardinal Ferdinand Dada, was invited and also several priests. ''Had I known *they* had been invited,'' writes Kiffin, ''I should hardly have parted with my £50!''

Also he was appointed Justice of the Peace and ''one of the lieutenancy,'' though he sought to join in only in matters that concerned the welfare of the city and the needs of orphans or others in distress.

Concerning William Kiffin's aldermanship the Ward of Cheap records read:

> *"October 27th, 1687.* This day Wm. Kiffen, Esq.,
> constituted by his Majesty alderman of the Ward of Cheap,
> did make his appearance before this court, and was here
> sworne (by virtue of his Majesty's writ of dedimus protestat)
> directed to this court, for the due execution of the said place."

On one occasion during his term of office "a precept
was prepared for preventing profanation of the Lord's
day." On another occasion help was given for poor French
Protestants in their worship. January 31st, 1687, records
a strange minute: "This court doth desire Mr. Alderman
Kiffin and Mr. Alderman Chamberlaine to sit upon the
green wax during the month of February next ensuing."
Did it mean something similar to the expression "sitting
on the woolsack," still used in Parliament today?

Kiffin was alderman for the Ward of Cheap, and was
highly respected during his term of office. After about nine
months he was able to gain, what to him was, his freedom.
So little did royal favours and earthly honours mean to
this man of God.

But deliverance from the despotic King and his desires
to overthrow Protestantism was at hand. Very soon the
"Glorious Revolution" was to take place. With the flight
of James II and the enthronement of William of Orange
a new era of toleration and liberty was to begin.
Concerning this Kiffin's comment expresses the feeling
of every true Protestant and every lover of liberty:

> "You all may see how good the Lord hath been to prevent
> those designs, then in hand, to destroy both our religion and
> our liberties, and I heartily desire that both myself and all
> others concerned may acknowledge the great goodness of
> God therein, that He may have the glory of all our delivering
> mercies."

And how true is Joseph Ivimey's appreciation of Kiffin
himself!:

"Seldom do we read such a deep tragedy in real life as that of this excellent man after the time that popish principles prevailed in the government; and seldom or never have we read of such firm and intrepid conduct in a man upwards of seventy years of age; whom no danger could terrify, no honours allure, nor any bribes blind his eyes or corrupt his hands."

CHAPTER 14

Kiffin and John Bunyan

Without doubt the best known religious figure of the seventeenth century was John Bunyan. It is obvious how in some ways there is a similarity between his life and that of William Kiffin's — though, of course, in many ways there was a vast difference. But here were two champions of nonconformity, suffering imprisonment for their faith. Obviously the question arises: as they lived at the same time, did they have any contact with each other? (Bunyan died in 1688, the year James II lost his throne.) Strangely, the contact that they did have with each other seems to be the only way in which Kiffin is known by many today; although it seems clear that in their lifetimes, it was Kiffin who was the one who was well-known.

We do not find that the two men ever met, though Bunyan often preached in London. Their contact came through a book which Bunyan published entitled *Differences in Judgement about Water Baptism no Bar to Communion, 1673*. Bunyan was not concerned whether a person partaking of the Lord's supper was baptized as an infant, or as a believer, or not at all. In his book he contends that the only qualification is to be a "a visible saint," that is, one who gives every appearance of being a true believer. Kiffin, however, felt that this was a very dangerous view, and contended that according to Scripture a person must not only be a true believer but must first be baptized by immersion. In other words, he was a Strict Baptist, believing in strict communion.

Though Bunyan's name is not even mentioned it has

always been agreed that the work Kiffin produced was in answer to Bunyan. It bore the title *A Sober Discourse of Right to Church Communion*, and was published in 1681, a small book of 163 pages (plus a preface and introduction), "London, Printed by Geo. Larkin, for Enoch Prosser, at the Rose and Crown in Sweethings Alley, at the East End of the Royal Exchange, 1681."

As this is the only book of any size that William Kiffin wrote, it is interesting to consider its contents. Not only does it give us an insight into Kiffin's abilities and his views, as well as his contact with John Bunyan, but the subject is one that still concerns us today.

On the title page the author signs himself "W. Kiffin a lover of Truth and Peace" and makes it plain that he "esteems them Christian brethren and saints" that he opposes, and that though he would debar those who were not baptized from the Lord's table, yet "not from our love and affection."

Kiffin makes it clear that he is not writing against Independents, Presbyterians or the Church of England; they practise infant baptism but they agree that this is necessary before coming to the Lord's table. His contention is with those Baptists who believe in believers' baptism by immersion as a scriptural ordinance, and who deny infant baptism, but who allow admission to the Lord's supper to a person unbaptized. It is equally clear that he feels exceedingly strongly on the subject.

One thing that seemed to concern him very deeply was that, if God has laid down an order in Scripture, then it is very solemn if we disregard it. It will be remembered how deeply burdened he was about this as a young man. Now, over forty years later, he still goes back to the case of Nadab and Abihu which affected him then:

> "You see how severe God was to Nadab and Abihu for but taking other fire than that which God appointed, to offer

up incense, though there was no direct commandment against it.''

Again he says:

"The least particle of divine truth being more valuable than anything the world can present.''

And he felt that it was so clearly revealed: belief, baptism, the Lord's supper — in that order.

But another thing also weighed heavily with him. If baptism is not necessary before coming to the Lord's table, then why do we exist as a separate body? Is there any real ground of separation from the Independents? Have the things we have suffered as Baptists been for nothing? And he himself had suffered much as a Baptist.

Moreover he went as far as to suggest that if it ever became a common opinion amongst Baptists that believers' baptism by immersion was scriptural but not needful before partaking of the Lord's supper, this would lead in time to the ordinance of baptism being despised and even falling into disuse.

He himself states:

"1. That God hath prescribed a particular way and method in which He will be worshipped.

"2. That He is so tender and nice therein that the least variation from His own stated order will not be allowed by Him, which appears by the punishment of such as transgressed and the praises given to such as kept His ordinances as they were delivered unto them.

"3. That to swerve from the Lord's institution, and invert His order, has had a direct tendency to destroy all modes of worship, and consequently all the solemn exercise of religion, inasmuch as the same reason by which one ordinance may be changed, or discontinued, will equally prove the change or discontinuance of any, yea all at long run.''

And Kiffin ever contended — BAPTISM — *after* faith; *before* any other ordinance.

Following an introduction "To the Christian reader" and a preface, there are five chapters which:

"1. State the question.

"2. Propose reasons why unbaptized persons may not be admitted to the Lord's supper.

"3. Produce some scripture demonstrations to evidence that such a practice (*viz.* so to admit them) is not evangelical.

"4. Show that it is against the practice and judgment of all Christians that have owned ordinances for above 1600 years.

"5. Answer objections."

His Scripture reasoning is very simple, concise and clear. In the New Testament we do not read of any believers who were not baptized, and their baptism usually followed soon after their belief. Acts 2.41 clearly gives the order: "Then they that gladly received His word were baptized: and the same day there were added unto them about three thousand souls." Also it is equally clear that all the New Testament churches were composed of baptized believers; Paul addresses them as consisting of those who were baptized. Also Kiffin states that in the New Testament baptism is emphasized *more* than the Lord's supper; but even if this were not so, it is wrong to exalt one ordinance at the expense of another.

In dealing with church history and the views of various learned writers, Kiffin reveals a remarkable knowledge, and also here and there quotes the original Greek (no mean attainment for one who as a poor orphan had little or no education!). It is interesting to find him quoting many of the well-known Puritans, his contemporaries. So we find

Owen, Goodwin, Coxe, Rogers, Burroughes, Bayne, Manton and others quoted. Of course, these believed in infant baptism; but Kiffin cites them, first, in support of the importance of a right order and, second, that there must be baptism before the Lord's supper or church membership (though in their case they understood the ordinance of baptism itself differently).

We meet with an interesting sideline here. Kiffin must have been well-acquainted with some of the leading Puritans, so we are interested to find him refer to ''the worthy and learned Dr. Owen'' and to speak of Jeremiah Burroughes so affectionately — ''that famous servant of God.... No man in his time (as those that knew him in his life can testify) was of a more tender and bearing spirit.'' (It was over forty years before that Burroughes had been made such a blessing to him.)

Kiffin makes himself very clear that he does not believe there is anything saving in ordinances; they are not necessary for salvation:

> ''I am well satisfied that the performance of all duties and ordinances will be of no value to any man further than Christ is enjoyed in them. The very gospel itself, severed from Christ, will prove the administration of death (2 Cor. 1.21). The powerfulest preaching and the clearest discourse of the free grace of God hath no life in it, unless the soul be led by the Spirit to Christ....Knowledge of the truth, and obedience to it in outward performances will as little save a man's soul as the covenant of works.''

Kiffin strongly felt that, out of love to Christ and to His people, he must show his brethren where he believed they were wrong as it was dishonouring to the Saviour:

> ''We labour to keep the Lord's ordinances in that purity and order the sacred records testify they were left in, and in a spirit of love and meekness to contend earnestly for the faith once delivered to the saints; which we conceive to be a duty enjoined upon all Christians.''

The thing that was thrown against William Kiffin more than anything else was that he was lacking in love. Where is the love of Christ when a dear child of God, who is sincere in his inability to see believers' baptism, is shut out and excluded from the Lord's supper which speaks of Christ's dying love?

To this Kiffin answers:

> "Yet, that cannot be called love which is exercised in opposition to the order prescribed in the Word, by which ordinances ought to be administered. For as love is a grace of the Spirit of Christ, so ordinances are the appointments of the same Spirit which works grace in the hearts of Christians; all true love being regulated by gospel-rule. And as all men may know the disciples of Christ by their love one to another, so also it is a character given by the same Lord of being a disciple when this love is manifest in keeping His commandments (John 14.15): 'If ye love Me, keep My commandments.'"

*   *   *

It is said that when Sir Peter Lely was painting Oliver Cromwell's portrait, he wished to omit the wart on his face. "Paint me warts and all!" was Cromwell's reply. So Kiffin's faults must not be excluded — if they can be proved.

Christopher Hill, whose recent book on Bunyan has been acclaimed "the book of the year," complains that Kiffin spoke very unkindly of John Bunyan. He says that in 1673 Bunyan was distressed because William Kiffin, whom he regarded as "my brother," despised his "person because of my low descent among men, stigmatising me for a person of *that* rank, that needed not to be heeded or attended to." Hill tells us that Kiffin declared "I had not meddled with the controversy at all, had I found any of parts that would divert themselves to take notice of *you*." Justifiably annoyed, Bunyan replied, "What kind of *you* am I? And why is *my* rank so mean, that the most gracious and godly among you may not duly and soberly consider of what I have said?'' Now, of course, there can be no excuse at all for speaking contemptuously of anyone, let alone a fellow-believer. However, in *A Sober Discourse* no trace of this appears. Kiffin's spirit seems very tender and loving. Witness:

> ''We propose on our judgment candidly and plainly without the least reflection upon or prejudice to our Christian brethren that dissent from us on this point, with whom and with all that can own the name of the Lord Jesus according to His gospel we desire to live in brotherly love and Christian society.''

But he adds:

> ''If we find our brethren entertain any unsound notion with respect to gospel truths, we look upon it as our duty to endeavour to inform them of it in a meek and sober way.''

Indeed, it is not absolutely certain that the words attributed to Kiffin were written by him; the book referred to *(Some Serious Reflections on That Part of Mr. Bunyan's Confession of Faith Touching Church Communion)* was written by Thomas Paul with the epistle to the reader written by Kiffin. Also, Kiffin's actual remarks can be read in different ways. Sadly a great deal of bitterness appeared in the controversy, proving that ''the best of men are only men at best.''

CHAPTER 15

Devonshire Square

What does seem sad is that so little is known of William Kiffin's ministry and the life of his congregation. We have so many details of his persecutions and imprisonments, his wealth and his honours, and even so much of his own gracious experience — but we know little of what took place in his church. Yet this was the most important part of his work.

For years his congregation met in Devonshire Square, Bishopsgate. Here in 1687 a large meeting house was erected, but before this it is clear that his congregation had met on this spot from the early years of his ministry.

Devonshire Square stands on the site of what was formerly known as Fisher's Folly. And the reason why is an interesting tale. In Tudor times there lived in London a wealthy goldsmith by the name of Jasper Fisher. Vanity apparently was his besetting sin for he had built for himself a sumptuous mansion, not many yards away from the Bishop's Gate. This was one of the finest homes in the old city, the spacious premises, the fine apartments, the costly fittings, the luxuriant gardens being the ''talk of the town.''

Really it was a piece of extravagant ostentation and at last Master Fisher became involved in debt, the mansion passing into the hands of the Earl of Oxford and later the Earl of Devonshire — hence Devonshire Square, built upon its ruins.

The building had become known as ''Fisher's Folly'' and so we find Kiffin's congregation in a satirical poem by Samuel Butler referred to as "Fisher's Folly congregation."

Whatever meeting house there was appears to have passed through various changes. At one time, after the Great Fire, it was used by the Church of England. The well-known Baptist historian, W.T.Whitley, states that the Particular Baptist congregation was excluded from Devonshire Square from 1669 onwards for a considerable number of years, meeting elsewhere in different places. A Sir Robert Titchbourne is reputed to have preached at Devonshire Square frequently at another time. This Titchbourne was one of the leading advocates for the death of Charles I and signed the warrant for his execution. He became a Member of Parliament and in 1655 was chosen Lord Mayor. After the Restoration he died in the Tower of London. What his connection with Kiffin was we do not know but apparently he was the author of an excellent piece of divinity, *A Cluster of Canaan's Grapes.** In later years Sir Gregory Page and his wife Dame Mary were regular worshippers at Devonshire Square and members there, probably before the death of Kiffin. On Dame Mary's grave in Bunhill Fields is the curious inscription:

> "In 67 months she was tap'd 66 times,
> Had taken away 240 gallons of water.
> Without ever repining at her case,
> Or ever fearing the operation."

More important they did all they could to help distressed nonconformists, distributing their wealth with a lavish hand.

The membership book of Kiffin's church makes it abundantly clear that he had a large congregation and that the church was made up of "all sorts and conditions of

---

*Wilson on *Dissenting Churches and Meeting Houses in London*, Vol. I., 1808, seems a little muddled on all this.

men'' — ''a shoemaker,'' ''a taylor,'' ''a mayd,'' ''a smith's wife,'' ''a talow chandler,'' ''a buttonmaker,'' ''a seller of fruite,'' ''a widdow,'' ''a silversmith's wife,'' ''a glassier,'' among them.

The meeting house (or chapel) in Devonshire Square, which survived till Victorian times, was opened on March 1st, 1687, in Meeting House Yard, Devonshire Square, Bishopsgate Street. The writer who records the opening services remarks: ''when Psalms were sung there.'' One of the great controversies among the seventeenth century Baptists was over whether congregational singing was scriptural or not. The point was not: should it be hymns or only Psalms? but: should there be any public singing at all? There were many arguments against but one was that it was wrong to put gracious words into the mouth of an unspiritual person. Another was that if objections were made to the Church of England using a book for prayer, it was wrong equally to use a book for singing. One suggestion was that it was scriptural to allow singing if the minister alone sang.

It seems that the Devonshire Square congregation was divided, like most others, and congregational singing was not regularly practised till the year that William Kiffin died. That was about the time Dr. Isaac Watts began his pastorate in London, and soon his version of the Psalms and then his hymns were being widely sung. But at Devonshire Square, in the beginning, the strange practice was followed which was fairly common in those days. In order to avoid dissension, at the end of the morning service those who did not believe in congregational singing quietly left, and those who did remained to sing a Psalm — all being done most amicably.

It is very clear that, as with all congregations in Puritan times, strict and gracious discipline was observed. The rule of Scripture was carefully followed, and no person guilty of walking contrary to Scripture was suffered to remain in membership. Thus we read of a member being cut off for frequenting the local Bishopsgate Church of England. Another was suspended for falsely representing himself as possessing a large sum of money (in order to gain the friendship of a young lady). A young woman was excommunicated for "keeping company with a parson of the Church of England." Another was cut off for distributing £200 of her husband's money. As far as possible it was to be ensured that the church consisted of godly souls. But it was not just negative. Visitors were appointed to provide quarterly reports of how the members were faring, and to help those in need. And the old account books make it abundantly clear how much money and time was spent on the needs of the poor. Again and again appears a list of subscribers — with "Bro. Kiffin" still at the top of the list with a generous subscription in August 1701, just before his death. (This, incidentally, is conclusive proof that the statement of some historians, that Kiffin's connection with Devonshire Square ended in 1693, is false.)

One important question concerning William Kiffin's pastorate needs to be answered: how did the church and congregation manage to continue (and even thrive) when their worthy pastor had such innumerable calls upon his time and talents? Happily, there is an easy answer. Kiffin was favoured with three eminently able and gracious assistant ministers (or co-pastors, or joint-elders, as they were sometimes known).

The first was Thomas Patient, sometimes called "Patience." At one time Patient was an Independent minister in New England but while there he became convinced of the rightness of the Baptist position. Not now being allowed to live quietly on the other side of the Atlantic, he returned to England in the early 1640s and became colleague with William Kiffin — though not formally ordained as pastor with him. Thus it was Thomas

Patient who, along with Kiffin, signed the 1644 Confession of Faith on behalf of the church at Devonshire Square.

After this he travelled about the country and went over to Ireland with General Fleetwood, Cromwell's son-in-law, at the time he became Lord Lieutenant. Patient was appointed to preach in the cathedral in Dublin and also became chaplain to Cromwell's brother-in-law, Colonel John Jones. Travelling round Ireland along with the English army, Patient's preaching appears to have been blessed and he was the founder of what became a very numerous church at Clough Keating.

Shortly after the Restoration, returning to England, he was chosen joint-elder with William Kiffin at Devonshire Square. In those times the services, setting aside a pastor for his work, were very lengthy and solemn. It was on June 28th, 1666, that Thomas Patient was so ordained, the ministers along with Kiffin being Hanserd Knollys and a Mr. Harrison.

Sadly, very soon afterwards Patient was removed by the hand of death, possibly by the plague. (If so, what memories this would bring back to Kiffin!) The church book records:

> "July 30, 1666, Thomas Patient was, on the 29th instant, discharged by death from his work and office, he being then taken from the evil to come, and having rested from all his labours, leaving a blessed savour behind him of his great usefulness, and sober conversation. This his sudden removal being looked upon to be his own great advantage, but the church's sore loss. On this day he was carried to his grave, accompanied by the members of this and other congregations, in a Christian, comely and decent manner."

The second assistant to Kiffin was a most learned man, Daniel Dyke, M.A. He was the son of one of the good old Puritan ministers, Jeremiah Dyke, and had himself been a minister in the established church after leaving Cambridge University. As a young man of great learning and also a useful preacher, he was soon presented to the valuable living at Hadham Magna (now, Much Hadham) in Hertfordshire. Coming to see that Baptist views were scriptural, he was still able to continue in Cromwell's days, being made a chaplain to the Lord Protector and also one of the Triers.

After the Restoration Daniel Dyke perceived his danger — a Baptist holding a living in the Church of England — and accordingly resigned. He had already tried to discourage those Puritan divines who thought that good days were in store with the coming of Charles II.

In 1667 (at the age of 50) he preached for a year on trial at Devonshire Square and was solemnly set apart as joint-elder on February 17th, 1668, the same three ministers taking part as at Patient's ordination. He is described as "a faithful labourer" and continued for twenty years with Kiffin, dying the same year as Bunyan, and being buried a few yards away from him.

The third assistant pastor to Kiffin was another former Church minister, Richard Adams. He too apparently was educated at Cambridge and became Vicar of Humberstone in Leicestershire. Being one of the ministers compelled to leave at the time of the Great Ejection, he preached in his own house to good congregations for fourteen years. At this time he was sorely persecuted by the neighbouring Justice of the Peace who fined him twelve pence a day. Yet so greatly was he respected that, when his pewter was seized as a punishment, no pewterer would buy it.

Later he moved to be a pastor in South London and, following the death of Daniel Dyke, he was ordained joint-elder with William Kiffin in October 1690. We are told "the service was managed with great solemnity," Hanserd Knollys, William Collins, Hercules Collins, and others, taking part. Mr. Knollys at that time was over 90 years of age, and it must have been one of his last public appearances. We are not told when Richard Adams adopted Baptist principles, but the peculiar importance which seems to have been attached to his ordination suggests that he may have been a recent "convert" to the denomination. One thing is clear: what little substance there is in the slanders that the old Particular Baptists were very ignorant and unlearned men!

After the death of Kiffin, Richard Adams continued as pastor.

CHAPTER 16

1689

1689 was a memorable year for England, and especially for those who had for so long suffered for their faith. The Glorious Revolution led to the Bill of Rights and the Toleration Act ensuring political and religious liberties. True, the nonconformists still had several disabilities — not for many years, for instance, were they permitted to enter university — but the days of cruel persecution were now ended. It was the time they had longed for, just as God's ancient people waited expectantly for the year of jubilee, "the acceptable year of the Lord."

So on January 2nd, 1689 we find William Kiffin leading a deputation of Baptists to present an address of welcome to William III and Mary. (We wonder if anyone else in the seventeenth century had personally met Charles I, Cromwell, Charles II, James II and William III!) Also Kiffin made a personal contribution towards the financial needs of William's government during its first six months.

For William Kiffin the Glorious Revolution meant that half a century's difficulties, trials, imprisonments were now at an end. *And, obviously, from this time his life is less exciting and interesting.*

The Baptists quickly made good use of their freedom, calling a General Assembly. It was made very clear that these were Baptists "denying Arminianism," Baptists "owning the doctrine of personal election and final perseverance." In other words these Particular Baptists owned only those churches which held the doctrines of grace, commonly called Calvinism. Neither were open membership churches, such as Bunyan's at Bedford, invited.

The Assembly which met from September 3rd to 11th must have been a remarkable gathering. Today it is specially remembered on account of the noble Confession of Faith which it issued, which was for many years the standard in Baptist churches.

The circular letter of invitation which was sent was signed by a few leading London ministers, and was headed by the signature of William Kiffin. Replies were to be sent to Hanserd Knollys (now 91 years old) or to William Kiffin "who lives in White's alley, Little Moorfields." They are described as "our reverend and well-beloved brethren." Each church was asked to send two messengers, the pastor and another; altogether over a hundred churches responded, from all over the country.

The letter (written by Kiffin?) made clear the sense of God's wonderful mercy which was felt:

> "We cannot but, first of all, adore the divine wisdom and goodness of Almighty God, in respect of His late most gracious providence, for our deliverance from that dismal dispensation, which threatened us from the continual and unwearied attempts and designs of the enemy of our sacred religion and civil liberties; by which means our sinking and drooping spirits are again revived, and our earnest hopes and long expectations raised."

However, there was much cause for confession and self-abasement:

> "We cannot but bewail the present condition our churches seem to be in; fearing that much of that former strength, life and vigour, which attended us is much gone; and in many places the interest of our Lord Jesus Christ seems to be much neglected which is in our hands, and the congregation to languish and our beauty to fade away (which thing, we have some ground to judge, you cannot but be sensible of as well as we)."

When September came these must have been wonderful meetings, everything done in an orderly fashion with a spirit of love and unity. How gratifying this must have been to William Kiffin as he contemplated the many changes that had taken place during the preceding fifty years!

A narrative of the proceedings was published, once more signed by Kiffin along with others. Again the spirit of gratitude for the recent wonderful deliverance is very marked:

> "We all see great cause to rejoice and bless God, that after so dismal an hour of sorrow and persecution, in which the enemy doubtless designed to break our churches to pieces, and not only us, but to make the whole Zion of God desolate, even so as she might become as a ploughed field; the Lord was pleased to give such strength and power in the time of need, to bear up your souls in your testimony for Jesus Christ, that your spirits did not faint under your burdens in the time of your adversity; so that we hope we may say, in the words of the church of old: 'Though all this is come upon us, yet we have not forgotten Thee, neither have we dealt falsely in Thy covenant. Our heart is not turned back, neither have our steps declined from Thy way. Though Thou hast sore broken us in the place of dragons, and covered us with the shadow of death' (Psa. 44.17,18,19)."

Again, too, there is the sense of unworthiness and self-abasement:

> "Yet nevertheless we fear Christ may say, 'I have somewhat against you, because you have left your first love,' as He once charged the church of Ephesus, and may possibly most churches in England; it is therefore good 'to consider from whence we are fallen, and repent and do our first works' (Rev. 2.5).
>
> "We are persuaded one chief cause of our decay is want of holy zeal for God, and the house of our God; few amongst us living up, we fear, to what they profess of God, nor

answering the terms of that sacred covenant they have made with Him; the power of godliness being greatly decayed, and but little more than the form thereof remaining amongst us. The thoughts of which are enough to melt our spirits, and break our hearts to pieces, considering those most amazing providences of the ever blessed God under which we have been, and more especially now are exercised, and the many signal and most endearing obligations He is pleased to lay us under. The spirit of this world, we clearly discern, has got too, too much into the hearts of most Christians and members of our churches, all seeking their own, and none or very few, the things of Jesus Christ; if therefore, in this there be no reformation, the whole interest of the blessed Lord Jesus will still sink in our hands, and our churches will be left to languish, whilst the hands of poor ministers become as weak as water, and sorrow and grief seize upon their spirits."

A fund was set up to help the various ministers and congregations, William Kiffin being one of "our honoured and well-beloved brethren" to receive the collection. Money had to be sent to Edward Harrison "living at the sign of the Hen and Chickens, in Cheapside, London," and another letter confirming it to Morice King, "living at the sign of the Mermaid in Lawrence Lane, silkman," who appears to have been one of Kiffin's members.

Though the Assembly strongly maintained the independency of the local church, it gave advice on several questions that had been submitted. "Our whole intendment is to be helpers together of one another by way of counsel and advice in the right understanding of that perfect rule which our Lord Jesus, the Bishop of our souls, hath thereby prescribed."

Some of the questions and answers are most interesting and profitable — for instance, concerning the keeping of the Lord's day, a subject dealt with very graciously and scripturally.

Most strongly did the Assembly pronounce against any

appearance of worldliness in the churches, believing that the grace of God will have a sanctifying effect in the life:

"It is a shame for men to wear long hair, or long periwigs, and especially ministers, 1 Cor. 11.14, or strange apparel, Zeph. 1.8. That the Lord reproves the daughters of Zion for the bravery, haughtiness and pride of their attire, walking with stretched out necks, wanton eyes, mincing as they go, Isa. 3.16. As if they affected tallness, as one observes upon their stretched-out necks; though some in these times seem, by their high dresses, to out-do them in that respect. The Apostle Paul exhorts in 1 Tim. 2.9,10, that 'women adorn themselves in modest apparel, with shamefacedness and sobriety: not with broidered hair, or gold, or pearls, or costly array; but with good works, as becometh women professing godliness.' And 1 Pet. 3.3.,4,5, 'Whose adorning let it not be the outward adorning of plaiting the hair, and of wearing of gold, or of putting on of apparel; but the ornament of a meek and quiet spirit, which is, in the sight of God, of great price: for after this' (fashion, or) 'manner, in old time, the holy women who trusted in God adorned themselves.' And therefore, we cannot but bewail it with much sorrow and grief of spirit, that those brethren and sisters, who have solemnly professed to deny themselves, Matt. 16.24, and who are by profession obliged in duty not to conform to this world, Rom. 12.2, should so much conform to the fashions of this world, and not reform themselves in those inclinations that their natures addicted them to in days of ignorance, 1 Pet. 1.14. From these considerations, we earnestly desire that men and women whose souls are committed to our charge, may be watched over in this matter, and that care be taken, and all just and due means used, for a reformation herein; and that such who are guilty of this crying sin of pride, that abounds in the churches as well as in the nation, may be reproved."

A General Fast was appointed for all the congregations to be held on October 10th. The causes and reasons were given, and again William Kiffin is one of the signatories (this time second, with Hanserd Knollys first). As some of the language is particularly beautiful, we give a lengthy extract:

"The main and principal evils to be bewailed and mourned over before the Lord on that day, are as follows:

"First, Those many grievous backslidings, sins and provocations, not only of the whole nation, but also of the Lord's own people, as considered in our public and private stations; particularly that great decay of first-love, faith and zeal for the ways and worship of God which hath been apparent, not only in our churches but also in private families.

"Secondly, That this declension and backsliding hath been, we fear, for a long series of time, and many sore judgments God has brought upon the nation; and a strange death of late come upon the Lord's faithful witnesses, besides divers painful labourers in Christ's vineyard called home and but few raised up in their stead; little success in the ministry; storms of persecution having been raised upon us; a new war commenced by the beast (through the permission of God and hand of His justice) to a total overcoming to appearance the witnesses of Christ in these isles; besides His more immediate strokes by plague and fire, etc. God not blessing all essays used for deliverance, so that we were almost without hope. Therefore our sins that provoked the righteous and just God to bring all these evils upon us, we ought to bewail and mourn for before Him. But withal, not to forget His infinite goodness who, when He saw that our power was gone and that there was none shut up or left, that He should thus appear for our help and deliverance in a way unexpected and unthought of by us.

"Thirdly, The things we should therefore in the next place pray and cry to the Lord for are, that He would give us true, broken and penitent hearts for all our iniquities and the sins of His people, and wash and cleanse away those great pollutions with which we have been defiled; and also pour forth more of His Spirit upon us and open the mysteries of His Word that we may understand whereabouts we are in respect of the latter time, and what He is a doing, and know our work, and that a blessing may attend all the churches of His saints in these nations, and that greater light may break forth and the glory of the Lord rise upon us, and that the Word may not any more be as a miscarrying womb and dry breasts, but that in every place multitudes may be turned to the Lord and that love and sweet concord may be found among all the Lord's people in these nations, that the great work begun therein so unexpectedly may go on and be perfected to the praise of His own glory.''

The relevance of all this in England today is clear. Consideration of the 1689 Assembly is not of mere academic interest.

CHAPTER 17

The 1689 Confession

But perhaps it is for issuing the Confession of Faith that the 1689 Assembly is best remembered today. What memories this must have brought back for William Kiffin, one of the signatories of the 1644 Confession forty-five years before!

In 1677 a new Confession had been compiled, and was "put forth by the Elders and Brethren of many Congregations of Christians (baptized upon Profession of their Faith) in London and the Country." There were no names given at the end of the Confession. (It was a time of persecution.)

The question may be asked: why a new Confession? What of the 1644 one? There appear to have been three reasons:

1. the scarcity of copies of the 1644 Confession. (Essential agreement is claimed between the two Confessions.)

2. the need for more full and distinct expression of their beliefs.

3. the necessity to confess "our hearty agreement with them (the Presbyterians and Independents) in that wholesome doctrine, which, with so clear evidence of Scripture they have asserted," and the Confessions they had issued.

The Confession the 1689 Assembly published is precisely the same as the 1677 Confession, though now signed by thirty-seven ministers on behalf of the whole Assembly. Knollys and Kiffin head the list. Very closely does the Baptist Confession follow the renowned Westminster Confession, which is still officially the standard for Presbyterian churches in Scotland. It will be remembered that the Westminster Assembly of Divines was appointed by Parliament and sat for a few years in the 1640s drawing up the Confession. Of course, the Baptist Confession differs from the Westminster on such matters as baptism. See "Chapter 29: BAPTISM":

"1. Baptism is an ordinance of the New Testament, ordained by Jesus Christ, to be unto the party baptized, a sign of his fellowship with Him, in His death and resurrection; of his being engrafted into Him; of remission of sins; and of his giving up to God, through Jesus Christ, to live and walk in newness of life.

"2. Those who do actually profess repentance towards God, faith in, and obedience to, our Lord Jesus Christ, are the only proper subjects of this ordinance.

"3. The outward element to be used in this ordinance is water, wherein the party is to be baptized, in the name of the Father, and of the Son, and of the Holy Spirit.

"4. Immersion, or dipping of the person in water, is necessary to the due administration of this ordinance."

The 1689 Confession went into many editions and later, as edited by Benjamin Keach and his son Elias, became the standard for Calvinistic Baptists in America, where it is known as "the Philadelphia Confession."

Altogether there are thirty-two chapters, each divided up (sometimes into nine or ten divisions). Proof texts are carefully given, and the whole is a remarkable body of divinity.

The Calvinism of the Confession is apparent:

"Chapter 3. 5: Those of mankind that are predestinated to life, God, before the foundation of the world was laid, according to His eternal and immutable purpose, and the secret counsel and good pleasure of His will, hath chosen in Christ unto everlasting glory, out of His mere free grace and love, without any other thing in the creature as a condition or cause moving Him thereunto.''

"Chapter 8. 5: The Lord Jesus, by His perfect obedience and sacrifice of Himself, which He through the eternal Spirit once offered up unto God, hath fully satisfied the justice of God, procured reconciliation, and purchased an everlasting inheritance in the kingdom of heaven for all those whom the Father hath given unto Him.''

Concerning the doctrine of the Trinity and of the Person of Christ the Confession is transparently clear, giving no precedent at all for those Calvinistic Baptists who in later years adopted such erroneous views on the Sonship of the Lord Jesus:

"Chapter 2. 3: In this divine and infinite Being there are three subsistences, the Father, the Word or Son, and Holy Spirit, of one substance, power and eternity, each having the whole divine essence, yet the essence undivided: the Father is of none, neither begotten nor proceeding; the Son is eternally begotten of the Father; the Holy Spirit proceeding from the Father and the Son; all infinite, without beginning, therefore but one God, who is not to be divided in nature and being, but distinguished by several peculiar relative properties and personal relations; which doctrine of the Trinity is the foundation of all our communion with God, and comfortable dependence on Him.''

"Chapter 8. 2: The Son of God, the second person in the Holy Trinity, being very and eternal God, the brightness of the Father's glory, of one substance and equal with Him who made the world, who upholdeth and governeth all things He hath made, did, when the fulness of time was come, take upon Him man's nature, with all the essential properties and common infirmities thereof, yet without sin; being conceived by the Holy Spirit in the womb of the Virgin Mary, the Holy Spirit coming down upon her: and the power of the Most High overshadowing her; and so was made of a woman of the tribe of Judah, of the seed of Abraham and David, according to the Scriptures; so that two whole, perfect and distinct natures were inseparably joined together in one person, without conversion, composition, or confusion; which person is very God and very man, yet one Christ the only mediator between God and man.''

CHAPTER 18

Last Days

Concerning William Kiffin's last days we do not know much. Following the Glorious Revolution and the 1689 General Assembly, he seems to have spent his last days in quietness. Surely he must have been worn out with his struggles and his sorrows. Though the point has been disputed, it seems clear that he remained the highly esteemed pastor of the same church right to the end — a period probably of over sixty years. "The most beloved Baptist of his times," he has been called.

Three other General Assemblies were held in London and at least one or two of them he was present. In 1692 he was even, with others, rebuked. The subject of congregational singing had long harrassed the churches. Would those who had written on the question (on each side) refer the matter to a small committee of seven? They agreed. Kiffin was one who *had* written on the subject — though we are not told on which side.

On May 24th, 1692, the committee issued their statement. Without saying which writers were right and which were wrong, it rebuked them all:

"How unlike to Jesus Christ, and the holy commands He hath given for brotherly love, your treatment hath been one towards another; who when He was reviled, reviled not again (1 Pet. 2.23). And how far short in this controversy you have come in answering that character which the Spirit of God gives of true charity (1 Cor. 13.4)! Had the things wherewith you charge each other been true, we humbly conceive you should have taken those rules which Christ hath prescribed

93

in a more private debate, way and method, that would not
have reflected upon your holy profession and the name of
God, to convince one another of your errors; and that the
ways you have taken to discover the nakedness of your
brethren have been irregular and tended rather to beget
greater offences and stumblings than convincing, healing and
recovering.''

How William Kiffin and the others reacted we are not
told. (The renowned Benjamin Keach, the introducer of
hymn singing in this country, was one of the others.)

In 1691 Kiffin's old friend, the worthy veteran Hanserd
Knollys, died. The next year his life was published with
the title:

> ''*The life and death of that old disciple of Jesus Christ and
> Eminent Minister of the Gospel, Mr. Hanserd Knollys, who
> died in the ninety-third year of his age*. Written with his own
> hand to the year 1672 and continued in general in an epistle
> by William Kiffin. London, 1692.''

Kiffin writes in the introduction: ''I have myself known
him for above fifty-four years.''

Knollys himself records an interesting episode:

> ''May 1670 (i.e. over 20 years before) had a short and
> powerful distemper in the bowels. No tongue can express
> my pains. Two learned, well-practised and judicious doctors
> of physic had daily visited me. God did not succeed their
> honest and faithful endeavours with His blessing. I resolved
> to take no more physic but would apply to that ordinance
> of God appointed by Jesus Christ the great Physician of value
> (James 5.14,15). And I got Mr. Kiffin and Mr. Vavasour
> Powell who prayed over me and anointed me with oil in the
> name of the Lord. And the Lord did hear prayer and heal
> me. For there were very many godly ministers and gracious
> saints that prayed day and night for me (with submission to
> the will of God), that the Lord would spare my life and heal
> me and make me more useful and serviceable to the Lord,
> to the church and to the saints whose prayers God had heard,

and as an answer to their prayer I was perfectly healed but remained weak long after.''

We mention this without comment. This is a day when many sweeping claims are made concerning the gifts of healing. We feel sure that William Kiffin would never have made such claims for himself. Only did he believe in the efficacy of prayer and the Lord's wonderful ability to answer.

Not long before he died Hanserd Knollys had said:

"My wilderness, sea, city and prison mercies afford me many and strong consolations. The spiritual sights of the glory of God, the divine sweetness of the presence of my Lord Jesus Christ, and the joys and comforts of the holy and eternal Spirit communicated to my soul, together with suitable and seasonable scriptures of truth, have so often and so powerfully revived, refreshed and strengthened my heart in the days of my pilgrimage, trials and sufferings that the sense, yea the life and sweetness thereof, abides still upon my heart; and hath engaged my soul to live by faith, to walk humbly and to desire and endeavour to excel in holiness to God's glory and the example of others. Though, I confess, many of the Lord's ministers and some of the Lord's people have excelled and outshined me, with whom God had not been at so much cost nor pains as He hath been with me. I am a very unprofitable servant, yet by the grace of God, I am what I am.''

It was a year later that William Kiffin completed the account of his own life which he had begun many years before. He wrote this specially for his children. He begins:

"It was one of the charges which God gave His people of old that those many great providences which they were made partakers of might by them be left to their children, to the end that they might from generation to generation be the more engaged to cleave unto the Lord. I have therefore thought it my duty to leave behind me some account of those many footsteps of His grace and goodness towards me; (being

95

now arrived to old age and by the many weaknesses and distempers which attend me, have cause to judge my time is not likely to be long in this world) — if it may contribute anything towards the provoking of your hearts to love, fear and obey that God who will never fail nor forsake those who trust in Him.''

In this account of the Lord's merciful dealings with him in providence and in grace we come close to the real William Kiffin. We penetrate the public figure, the wealthy merchant, the eminent pastor, the successful disputant, and come face to face with a man of great humility and tenderness of heart, one well taught by the Spirit of God and established in the truth.

With what affection does he write:

"Being now sensible of the decays of nature and the great inability that attends me thereby to do service for Jesus Christ, the counsel I would leave with you is; First, have a care of your hearts that they be not taken with the vanities of this present evil world. Your temptations may be more than mine were in my younger days, in regard that your means of enjoying the world are much more. But yet consider it is an evil requital to the Lord for the mercies shewn to your father; that what God hath given him and hath been left by him to you, should be used to sin against that God who hath freely given it. O! let not that which your father hath received as mercy from God be so used that at last it may prove a curse to you.

"I have often prayed from the hands of God that you may have another portion than the world in this life: that Christ may be your portion and that your younger years may be spent in looking after that one thing necessary. This hath been the desire of my soul to God for you. I well know outward mercies prove great snares to keep many from Christ and call for great watchfulness over our hearts in the enjoyment of them. We are very apt to follow example, therefore we are counselled not to follow a multitude to do evil. Our Lord Christ tells us that 'broad is the way that leads to destruction and many there be that find it.' This broad way men need not to be taught; the corruption of their hearts and the subtility of Satan soon points it out.''

Writers of Baptist history have obviously referred continually to Kiffin's own account of his life. Sometimes there has been amazement expressed at things omitted, and sometimes a difficulty in establishing facts or exact dates. Really, though, the old man's desire was not a concise autobiography. Rather was it to speak of some of God's dealings with him, especially the remarkable providences which would interest them. Then it is not surprising that it is not a polished, well-documented account.

This manuscript was handed down in the family till in the 1820s a lineal descendant, Richard Frost of Dunmow, Essex, lent it to both William Orme and Joseph Ivimey, who published it (or most of it) in different formats. The original was signed:

> ''The following short account of my great, great, great grandfather, William Kiffin, was wrote by himself in his advanced year bearing date 1693, and was copied by myself from his own handwriting here in London, March 1764.
> R. Frost.''

There were still one or two storms before William Kiffin entered the haven. In 1698 his son Harry, who, was only 44, was removed by death, and it is probable that Mrs. Henrietta Catcher who died the same year, aged only 22, and was buried in the same grave, was a granddaughter.

What is clear is that Kiffin's noble generosity remained unchanged right down to old age. The Huguenot family which had fled from France, and which he had supported at his own expense, recovered some of its former wealth with the passing of time. But the old man ''would not diminish it a single shilling by taking any retribution for the services he had rendered them.''

William Kiffin lived on into the next century, dying peacefully (not long before King William III) on December 29th, 1701. He was 85. A quiet end to a stormy and eventful life! Is the title *Stranger than Fiction* an exaggeration? We think not. And surely not the least remarkable thing is that Kiffin should come safely through so many things, live to a ripe old age, and then die peacefully at last. Never let it be forgotten that it was the infamous Judge Jeffreys who longed to see him on the gallows. And Jeffreys usually gained his end.

Concerning Kiffin's funeral we know nothing. Who buried him? His old friend Knollys was already gone. Could it have been the well-known Benjamin Keach? Or would it have been his own co-pastor, Richard Adams? Often a funeral sermon was published following the death of a respected pastor, but we have no trace of one on this occasion.

We have, however, an interesting account of what took place some years later when one of William Kiffin's successors at Devonshire Square was buried. Usually such occasions were managed with much solemnity. The church book recorded that it was agreed:

"1. That the corpse be carried from the meeting house, and interred in the burial ground, Bunhill Fields, on Monday, 27th instant.

"2. That a sermon be preached on the occasion by Mr. Richardson, to begin at four o'clock precisely.

"3. That Mr. Noble, or Mr. Wallin, be desired to pronounce a funeral oration at the grave.

"4. That the following ministers be invited to support the pall. (Here six names follow.)

"5. That the following pastors and ministers be also invited. (Here fourteen names follow.)

"6. That hatbands, gloves and cloaks be provided for all the ministers.

"7. That all the brethren are desired to provide themselves

hatbands, gloves and cloaks, for their more decent attendance at the funeral.''

It can be assumed that Kiffin's funeral took place with similar solemnity. William Kiffin was buried in the old London nonconformist burial ground, Bunhill Fields, where the dust of so many of the old divines lie — Bunyan, Owen, Goodwin, Dr. Watts, Hanserd Knollys, and many others. Not only has the headstone disappeared but the spot is completely unknown; even 140 years ago. J.A.Jones in his *Bunhill Memorials* had no tradition of where it could be found.

Strype, in his edition of Stow's *Survey of London*, however, has preserved details of the inscription on the grave. Obviously the third line (in brackets) is Strype's own insertion.

WILLIAM KIFFIN

Eldest son of William Kiffin, of London, Merchant,
(and an Anabaptist Preacher,)
Died in the Lord, August 31st, 1669,
In the 21st year of his age.

Also

PRISCILLA LIDDEL
Wife of Robert Liddel.
And daughter of William Kiffin,
Who fell asleep in the Lord, March 15, 1679.
Aged 24.

And

HANNA, late Wife of William Kiffin,
And Mother to the above named William and Priscilla,
Who fell asleep in the Lord, the 6th October, 1682
In the 67th year of her age.

And

HARRY KIFFIN
Son of the above said William Kiffin,
Dec. 8, 1698, aged 44.

Also

HENRIETTA, late Wife of John Catcher,
August 15, 1698, aged 22.

And

WILLIAM KIFFIN, the Elder,
Of London, Merchant,
Husband to the above said Hanna,
And Father to the above said William, Harry and Priscilla,
Dec. 29, 1701,
In the 86th year of his age.

CHAPTER 19

Epilogue

As we come to the end of William Kiffin's remarkable life, we stand amazed that he was brought safely and honourably through. His own testimony, at the end of his life was:

> "That God, who hath given me occasion to trust in Him ever since I lay upon my mother's breast, and hath carried me along under many changes of my life, hath wonderfully wrought for me, and preserved me by His grace to this moment."

But what can we learn from Kiffin's life? What has he to say to us today? It will soon be 300 years since he died, and yet there are many similarities in our own turbulent age to his own.

One thing that the life of William Kiffin has to say to us is that God is able, when it pleases Him, to raise up men in positions of the greatest influence in our land. We think of Joseph being raised up to a position of influence in Egypt and Daniel in Babylon; in a similar though smaller way Kiffin was involved with statesmen and kings, and was able to use his influence for the good of God's people. Yet in reality he never was a politician nor interested either in politics or in seeking a name for himself.

But, secondly, we see how it is possible for a man, as upheld by God, to maintain his integrity amid ten thousand temptations. Again we think of how Daniel continued steadfastly for about seventy years with changing governments and monarchs.

Few have had both the temptations of adversity and

prosperity as Kiffin had. Abuse, accusations, arrest, imprisonment; and then wealth, honour, influence at court — but none of these things moved him. His contemporaries, the eminent Puritan divines, used to comment that many who stood the trial of adversity fell in the trial of prosperity; that if adversity slew its thousands, prosperity slew its tens of thousands. But Kiffin continued to the end a humble, godly, tender-hearted child of God, loved by God's people and respected and esteemed by the world.

Then, thirdly, we learn God's wonderful ability to deliver, however impossible the circumstance may be — and this not once or twice, but continually. We are reminded how the Apostle Paul once gave a catalogue of his trials and distresses, and added, "But out of them all the Lord delivered me."

There is a fourth thing. William Kiffin's whole life was governed by the Bible, the Word of God. In his early days he was deeply concerned as to what is the right order in the church, how God is to be worshipped. It seemed to be burned into his heart that God has laid down a pattern for His church, and that it is solemn to deviate from it. So he was led to the doctrines of grace (or Calvinism); then to a belief that baptism must be for believers only by immersion in water; and then that only those so baptized were permitted to the Lord's supper.

We live in an ecumenical age. Even God's people are tempted with the thought: if things in the world are so dreadful, is it right to contend so strongly for things on which God's people are not united? Kiffin stood in no uncertainty here. He felt that if he deviated in any measure from what he believed was the order God Himself had laid down, God would be dishonoured. (Is this the reason why he has been neglected in recent years, and so little heard of?)

Obviously, not all agree with his conclusions; but is not

God's order in the church important? and should we not seek, whatever the cost, to follow what we believe God has ordained?

We cannot forbear from pausing to think what William Kiffin might have been had he been willing to compromise or to conform. Would he have been offered one of the highest positions in the Government? Or would he have become a Bishop, or even an Archbishop? Well, we do not know. Through God's mercy it was always his desire to be identified with the poor, despised people of God. The scripture which seems most applicable to his interesting life is: ''Choosing rather to suffer affliction with the people of God, than to enjoy the pleasures of sin for a season; esteeming the reproach of Christ greater riches than the treasures in Egypt: for he had respect unto the recompence of the reward.''

William Kiffin was not unconcerned about future generations, though he could not possibly have envisaged our times. Let his last word to us be the message he left for his children, grandchildren and great-grandchildren at the end of his own account of his life:

''I have tasted of the goodness of God and His favour towards me from my youth, it being now sixty years since it pleased the Lord to give me a taste of His rich grace and mercy in Jesus Christ to my soul. Although my unprofitableness under these mercies and providences that have attended me hath been very great, they are not to be looked upon as products of chance (as many do serve experiences and deliverances, which they receive from God in the course of their lives) but as fruits of the care and goodness which God is pleased to show His poor people, while they are in this world; as there is no desire hatched against them for their ruin but they are rescued from them by the special care and providence of God. And truly I may say by experience, 'If the Lord had not been my help, they would many a time have swallowed me up quick.'

''I leave these few instances of the divine care to you my

children, grandchildren and great-grandchildren that you may remember them with thankful heart as they must prove to the praise of God on my account. I leave them, also, desiring the Lord to bless them to you, above all praying for you that you might in a special manner look after the concerns of your souls. To know God and Jesus Christ is eternal life. Endeavour to be diligent, to enquire after and to be established in the great doctrines of the gospel, which is of absolute necessity to salvation.

"I must every day expect to leave the world having lived in it much longer than I expected, yet I know not what my eyes may see before my change. The world is full of confusion. The last times are upon us. The signs are very visible. Iniquity abounds, and the love of many in religion waxes cold. God is by His providence shaking the earth under our feet. *There is no sure foundation of rest and peace but only in Jesus Christ.* To His grace I commend you. Amen."

Kiffin's Only Published Sermon

We feel it will be of interest to give the substance of the only record we have of a sermon which William Kiffin preached. (All parts in quotation marks are the exact words Kiffin spoke, apart from the modernising of spelling and punctuation, and Bible quotations.)

Text: "And she shall follow after her lovers, but she shall not overtake them; and she shall seek them, but shall not find them: then shall she say, I will go and return to my first husband; for then was it better with me than now. For she did not know that I gave her corn, and wine, and oil, and multiplied her silver and gold, which they prepared for Baal" (Hosea 2. 7,8).

First of all there is an introduction, explaining the context.

Next the preacher sets out his four points:

"I. The strength of these people's spirits in cleaving to affect her lovers, expressed in these words, *following after them and seeking them*.

"II. The means which the Lord here useth to reclaim her from them, expressed in these words, *though she do seek after them, yet she shall not find them*: she shall be disappointed of her ends herein.

"III.The effect that this means wrought (by the blessing of God upon it) expressed in these words, *then she shall say, I will return to my first husband*, etc.

"IV. Here is laid a main motive or consideration that wrought upon her spirit expressed in the latter clause of the verse, *for then* (saith she) *it was better with me than now.*"

The substance of the sermon is as follows:

I. Why this comes to pass:

Reason 1. Because the terms which other gods propound are more suitable to men's carnal reasoning. On the other hand with the true God it is: "Foxes have holes, and birds of the air have nests; but the Son of man hath not where to lay His head" — which the flesh does not like. "They must suffer for His name's sake."

Reason 2. Because men have more commerce with the world, sin and false worship. They are like Demas (2 Timothy 4.10). "Where your treasure is, there will your heart be also." The opposite is "to behold the loveliness and glory, fulness and excellency that is in Jesus Christ." "A bundle of myrrh is my well-beloved unto me; He shall lie all night betwixt my breasts."
"O saith the soul, Christ shall have the chiefest seat of residence in my heart.... What though I am imprisoned, reproached, disgraced, counted a sectious person, one that troubleth the state, yet this is no trouble at all unto such a heart, for he looks up to Christ, desiring with Him to endure the cross, and despise the shame."

Reason 3. Even the saints have that in them which will go after other gods. Satan seeks this, and at times they neglect their spiritual watchfulness. David is a solemn example of this.

II. When God will reclaim a fallen saint or bring a sinner for the first time to a knowledge of Himself, "the usual way that He takes herein is to discover to them the emptiness and insufficiency of all things that are here below, as not being able to give any content or satisfaction to the soul.''

In verse 14 he speaks of the wilderness, where He brings them, ''having neither penny nor pennies' worth — Isaiah 55.1.'' So in Jeremiah 3.23: ''Truly in vain is salvation hoped for from the hills, and from the multitude of mountains: truly in the Lord our God is the salvation of Israel.'' So Solomon learned that, ''Vanity of vanities: all is vanity.''

As long as the soul sees any fulness, either in heaven or earth out of Christ, it will ''fasten at the horns of that altar.'' Thus Jacob, while there was corn in Canaan, found no need to go into Egypt.

But God cuts off everything ''that so the soul may see Jesus Christ to be He who has all the wellsprings of comfort, and peace, and joy, and refreshment to the soul.''

Use 1. Let us examine ourselves. Is it the world? ''or whether the excellent fulness and goodness that is in Jesus Christ?'' ''If any man love the world, the love of the Father is not in him.''

Has God made us this discovery: ''that all the things of the world are empty and poor and weak, not able to give out the least dram of true comfort to the soul''? ''We cannot serve God and Mammon.'' We cannot play fast and loose with Christ.

''Wherefore let us not rest satisfied with a face of profession, but let us labour to make enquiry into our own heart and see what discoveries God hath made to us of the creature's emptiness and His own fulness.''

Use 2. The Lord strips of everything so that His people may see more fulness, ''yea even all fulness in Himself.''

The world cannot understand God's dealings with His people; they regard them as poor and mean. But,

"Hearken, my beloved brethren, Hath not God chosen the poor of this world rich in faith, and heirs of the kingdom which He hath promised to them that love Him?"

"This is a thing worthy of serious attention, that God should choose poor nothings of this world to be rich in faith and heirs of the kingdom."

"Usually the meaner the saints' conditions in the world, the fuller and richer are they in faith, and in communion with Jesus Christ."

If God sorely afflicts us and should take away even our wife and children, we should labour to make use of it "to see more fulness in Him from whom we have all our mercies."

III. The fruit: to return — it does not say to a Saviour but to a husband; that is, to yield subjection and obedience. "Jesus Christ is the only Head and Husband, Lord and Lawgiver of His church and people."

See Ephesians 1.22,23; Ephesians 4.15,16; Ephesians 5.23; Colossians 1.18; and Isaiah 33.22.

Reason 1. The church was taken out of the side of Christ as Eve was out of the side of Adam. But the church fell in Adam, "and so had continued, had not Jesus Christ stepped between the misery of the creature and the wrath of His Father, and by His own blood made up that great breach which sin had made between the creature man and the great Creator the Lord of heaven and earth. Had it not been for Christ, there had not so much as the name of a church of God been heard upon the face of the earth."

As Adam claimed propriety in Eve (Kiffin calls her "Hevah") because taken from his side, so Jesus Christ with His church.

Reason 2. Because Jesus Christ has bought His church: they are "the travail of His soul." "Seeing Christ hath satisfied God His Father by His own blood, is it not reason that we should live to His praise and honour?''

Kiffin then uses the interesting analogy: what would we think if a mother had a most difficult time in the birth of a child, and then a stranger should snatch away that child and demand it as her own?

Use 1. All that act this way are reproved. Though men labour to dethrone Christ, the time is coming when He will dethrone all His enemies. His enemies shall be His footstool.

Therefore it is terrible when men prescribe rules for the government of Christ's church, ''step up in Christ's stead.'' Christ Himself has prescribed pure and perfect laws for His church, and His people should be subject to them.

Use 2. How wonderful and singular is the love of Jesus Christ as Head and Husband toward a company of poor creatures!

Why should there be such a near relation — husband and wife? There is no reason in Christ why He should love us; there is every reason in us why He should loathe us.

What is the reason? Mercy! Hosea 2.19: ''I will marry thee to Myself in mercy and compassion.'' ''It has been the mere mercy and compassion of Jesus Christ working in His own breast that hath brought this great and mighty work to pass.''

If we seriously consider this, ''it would cause us to be willing to be anything, to do anything, yea to suffer anything for Him, who hath been and done and suffered so much for us.''

Use 3. We should yield subjection to Jesus Christ and His laws in all things.

   i. It must be *free* subjection. It must flow from the

consideration of the excellency that is in Christ and His laws "and from no other end whatsoever."

So David in Psalm 119.94: "I am Thine, save me; for I have sought Thy precepts" — I seek them merely for their excellency.

Many outwardly subject themselves but seek Him for the loaves and the fishes, "for their own by-ends and respects."

ii. It must be *universal*. "Christ calls for all" — Mark 12.33. "Ye are bought with a price: therefore glorify God in your body, and in your spirit, which are God's."

iii. It must be *perpetual*. "Be thou faithful unto death, and I will give thee a crown of life." God is to be served "all the days of our life" (Luke 1.74,75).

"If we do but cast our eye upon Christ, we shall see that which may engage us hereunto: as Christ's love was a free love; secondly, it was a full love, and thirdly, it was a durable love. Whom He loves once He loves to the end."

Use 4. Consolation to those governed by Christ's sceptre.

Is Christ your Husband?

i. He will provide for you. (Psalm 34.10; Isaiah 54.4,5.)

ii. Protection. "All His saints are in Thy hand."

"He will either keep His people from trouble, or support them in trouble." (Isaiah 43.2; Isaiah 63.10.)

iii. Preservation. "I will never leave thee, nor forsake thee." "Because I live ye shall live also." "But Zion said, the Lord hath forsaken me, and my Lord hath forgotten me. Can a woman forget her sucking child, that she should not have compassion on the son of her womb? yea, they may forget, yet will I not forget thee. Behold, I have graven thee upon the palms of My hands; thy walls are continually before Me."

"As if He should say, it's as possible for men to pull

110

away My strength from Myself as to pull away My people from Me, which seems to be held out in these words, 'I have engraven thee upon the palms of My hands.' That which is engraven in a man's hands is, as it were, made one with the hand; you may as well pull away the part of the hand as the engraving in the hand. So indeed are the people of God interested in that great attribute of God's strength, that men and devils may as soon pull God out of heaven as the saints out of God's hands.''

IV. The motive: the goodness she had formerly found in God's ways was better.

''That is ever best with the servants of God and churches of Christ when they keep closest to God.''

''I remember thee, the kindness of thy youth, the love of thine espousals, when thou wentest after Me in the wilderness, in a land that was not sown'' (Jeremiah 2.2). Did they lose anything? No. See verse 3: ''Israel was holiness unto the Lord and the firstfruits of His increase: all that devour him shall offend; evil shall come upon them, saith the Lord.'' Terrible if any oppose God's people!

See Exodus 19.5; Jeremiah 7.23.

It has always been well with the saints when they have walked in the ways of God:

Reason 1. Because kept by God from disaster and sorrow and shame and confusion that seize those that forsake Him.

See Psalm 119.4; Psalm 99.4; Jeremiah 3.2.

''It hath been well with the saints when they have closely walked in the ways of God.''

What makes men ashamed and confounded? When frustrated in their hope and expectation. But God's people shall *not* be frustrated of the promise. Though they know reproaches, scoffs, imprisonment, yet these should be their honour and joy.

Reason 2. Because those who keep closest to God are most honoured of God.

"It's sin that brings shame and confusion of face, but when the soul walks closely with its God, it shall be sure to be kept from shame."

Those churches since Christ's coming which have been most holy have been most persecuted. See Revelation 2.9,10: the church at Smyrna.

Reason 3. Because kept from distracting fears in the time of danger. "He shall not be afraid of evil tidings: his heart is fixed, trusting in the Lord."

See Psalm 23.3,4.

"And truly it is no small privilege, (especially in times of fears) to be kept and secured from fears."

Use 1.

"Let us then who profess the name of Christ, and appear to be in the number of those who are made nigh unto God by the blood of Christ, let us be exhorted to take heed of backsliding."

i. It is an easy thing to backslide because of the deceitfulness of our hearts, the snares of the world, and the subtleness of Satan.

ii. It is a dangerous thing to backslide:

a. *From* what we backslide — God.

b. *To* whom we backslide — that which is not able to relieve us or help us in trouble.

c. What God's carriage is to backsliders. "He shall be filled with his own ways." "If any man draw back, My soul shall have no pleasure in him."

A. *Some signs of a soul declining from God.*

1. A disregarding of the truth of Christ. 2 Chronicles 24.20.

2. Men grow distrustful of God and His truth; that is, when many things God has said seem hard. In John 6.60

they thought it "a hard saying"; then they drew back.

3. Unfruitfulness under the means and mercies. Luke 3.7. Men turn the truth of God into nothing; they please themselves more with talking of truth than practising it.

4. Love of the world. Men's spirits hanker after the world.

"He that loves the world had rather lose Jesus Christ than the world, and it must needs be so, because he loves it."

5. Spiritual pride, self-confidence. "Before destruction the heart is haughty."

"When a man is proud of that which is not his own, it's no marvel if he soon prove a spiritual bankrupt."

LET US LOOK TO OURSELVES. "Let him that thinketh he standeth take heed lest he fall."

B. *Some measures to prevent it.*

1. Let us labour for soundness of judgment in the truth of God. "Prove all things: hold fast that which is good."

"Ignorance is the mother of error, and a corrupted life doth soon follow an erroneous judgment."

Let us search the Scriptures, seek God in prayer "that He would be pleased to unfold those glorious mysteries of His will in His Word unto us by His Spirit, that so we may be able to judge of things that differ."

2. Let us labour to receive the truth in the love of it. Love will do it. What did God's love do (John 3.16)? Love will enable us to labour and to suffer.

"If once the love of our souls be given up to the excellency of the truth, then our lives, our liberties, our estates, our friends will follow roundly, but if there be a defect in our love to the truth, there will soon be a defect in our standing too, or suffering for truth."

3. Let us consider that the truth of God is the portion of the saints. "If we lose truth we lose Jesus Christ." Proverbs 4.13.

See David and his attitude to God's Word: Psalm 119.49,50,92. This was his companion in trouble.

The world reckons itself by what it has in the world, the people of God by what they have in Christ.

See Naboth: 1 Kings 21.3,4.

William Kiffin then goes on to the 8th verse: "For she did not know that I gave her corn, and wine, and oil, and multiplied her silver and gold, which they prepared for Baal." He states his main point: the main reason for decline — not taking notice of God's mercies.

Then follow the formal divisions:

I. The mercies: "corn and wine."

II. The Author of mercies: "I gave them" — God.

III. The persons to whom these mercies were given — "the children of Israel."

IV. The carriage of the people to God in the enjoyment of these mercies.

1. They took no notice from what hand they came: "for she did not know that I gave her corn," etc.

2. In spending them, they took not notice of where they go: "which they prepared for Baal."

On this 8th verse Kiffin is very brief. Was his time gone? (The sermon must have taken two hours to preach.) Or had he not time in prison preparing it for the press? Or had the pamphlet to be kept to a certain size, and the end is but a summary? We do not know.

However immediately follow three observations:

Observation 1. God is the only giver of every mercy and favour.

Observation 2. It is the duty of the saints to take special notice of God's mercies and favours.

Observation 3. Not taking notice of God's mercies and

114

favours is a special means to cause men to depart from God.

As concerning Observation 1, none will deny this. James 1.17.

"If we have any riches, any honours, any friends, any grace, any gifts, all come from God. And therefore we should take heed of sacrificing anything to our own nets, but as all mercies we receive come from God, so we must give the glory of all only to Him, who is only worthy of all honour and glory and praise for ever."

"These being the observations and this the substance of all the matter which God was pleased to help me to deliver where I was apprehended, as I am publicly called by many to suffer for them, so I am not unwilling, being requested to declare them to all, to such, and unto any it pleaseth God of His good providence to dispose of them, desiring that all persons would 'prove all things, and hold fast that which is good' (1 Thessalonians 5.21)."

A good end to a good sermon! And what a sermon it is — especially when we remember that it was preached by a young man of 25 or 26 without any formal education and no ministerial training! We see a sound knowledge of divinity, a right dividing of the Word, and a gracious application.

At the end Kiffin makes a statement of his reasons for publishing the sermon, and the whole concludes with two texts:

"For I am not ashamed of the gospel of Christ: for it is the power of God unto salvation to every one that believeth" (Romans 1.16).

"Be not thou therefore ashamed of the testimony of our Lord, nor of me His prisoner: but be thou partaker of the afflictions of the gospel" (2 Timothy 1.8).

Letter by Benjamin Hewling

The following letter was written by Benjamin Hewling to his mother about two hours before his death. See page 60.

Taunton, 30th September, 1685

Honoured Mother,

That news which I know you have a long while feared, and we expected, I must now acquaint you with, that, notwithstanding the hopes you gave in your two last letters, Warrants are come down for my execution, and within these few hours I expect it to be performed. Blessed be the Almighty God, that gives comfort and support in such a day. How ought we to magnify His holy name for all His mercies, that when we were running on in a course of sin, He should stop us in our full career, and shew us that Christ, whom we had pierced; and out of His free grace enable us to look upon Him with an eye of faith, believing Him able to save to the uttermost all such as come to Him. O! admirable long-suffering and patience of God, that when we were dishonouring His name, He did not take that time to bring honour to Himself by our destruction. But He delighteth not in the death of a sinner, but had rather he should turn to Him and live. He has many ways of bringing His own to Himself. Blessed be His holy name, that through affliction He has taught my heart to be in some measure conformable to His will, which worketh patience, and patience worketh experience, and experience hope, which maketh not ashamed.

I bless God, I am not ashamed of the cause for which I lay down my life, and as I have engaged in it and fought for it, so now I am going to seal it with my blood. The Lord still carry on the same cause which hath been long on foot! And though we die in it and for it, I question not but in His own due time He will raise up other instruments, more worthy to carry it on to the glory of His name, and the advancement of His church and people. Honoured mother, I know there has been nothing left undone by you or my friends, for the saving of my life, for which I return many hearty acknowledgements to yourself and them all; and it is my dying request to you and them, to pardon all undutifulness and unkindness in every relation.

Pray give my duty to my grandfather and grandmother, service to my uncles, and aunts, and my dear love to all my sisters; to every relation and friend a particular recommendation. Pray tell them all how precious an interest in Christ is, when we come to die, and advise them never to rest in a Christless state; for if we are His, it is no matter what the world do to us. They can but kill the body, and blessed be God, the soul is out of their reach. For I question not, but their malice wishes the damnation of that as well as the destruction of the body; which has too evidently appeared by their deceitful, flattering promises.

I commit you all to the care and protection of God, who has promised to be a father to the fatherless, and a husband to the widow, and to supply the want of every relation. The Lord God of heaven be your comfort under these sorrows, and your refuge from the miseries we may easily foresee coming upon poor England, and the poor distressed people of God in it. The Lord carry you through this vale of tears with a resigning, submissive spirit, and at last bring you to Himself in glory; where, I question not, but you will meet your dying son,

BENJAMIN HEWLING

117